Women Afire!

LIVING WITH MEANING AND PURPOSE MIDLIFE AND BEYOND

Charlotte Eliopoulos RN, MPH, ND, PhD

This book is dedicated to the many incredible examples of Women Afire who have touched my life and demonstrated lives of purpose and passion and to my husband, George Considine, for his support and encouragement.

I offer special appreciation to:
Jeannie Arnold
Lori Gutierrez
Gail Pohl
Sandra Sanders
Lorraine Seelaus
M.E. Shehata
Susan Wickard
and
Nancy Young
for their willingness to review and offer suggestions on the manuscript and, most importantly, for being awesome examples of Women Afire!

Women Afire!

LIVING WITH MEANING AND PURPOSE
MIDLIFE AND BEYOND

Table of Contents

Preface

We must be willing to get rid of the life we've planned,
so as to have the life that is waiting for us. The old skin
has to be shed before the new one can come.
~Joseph Campbell~

On a dreary, dark wintry afternoon that matched my mood perfectly, I found myself plopped in my family room's recliner with a meandering mind. *Should I change the color of the room? I really need to respond to those emails. What time is the meeting I'm supposed to attend this evening? Maybe we should move to the city. I haven't talked to Tina for awhile. Who was I supposed to phone? Am I getting too old to effectively stay competent in my profession? There really is too much clutter around this house.* My thoughts were everywhere but on the project that begged for attention on my desk. To my frustration---and concern---this distracting state of skipping through a foggy mental maze was not new or unusual for me these days. Just another one of the joys of menopause!

As I glanced around the room my eyes rested on a curio cabinet that housed a collection of old Snow White and the Seven Dwarfs composition dolls. These little figures had sat on the shelf for years but today they had new meaning for me as I began to see how they reflected my menopausal state. My reduced energy level and daytime drowsiness from sleep disturbances helped me to identify with *Sleepy*. *Sneezy* reminded me of the new aches, pains, and sensitivities I was experiencing. My cloudy, foggy mind found a sympathetic friend in *Dopey*. The change from my youthful arrogance to periodic lack of confidence (particularly when among bright, young, attractive women!) helped me to relate to *Bashful*. There were times I felt wise and able to offer valuable aid to others, much like *Doc*, but there probably were just as many times that my superb execution of the role of *Grumpy* drove others up a wall. There were blessings that I couldn't begin to appreciate in younger years that gave me joy and an affinity to *Happy*. And then there were times, in the private corners of my mind, that I still saw myself like *Snow White*, an innocent pretty young girl rather than a wrinkled crone who had more than a half century under her belt. Who would have thought that these little fairy tale creatures could symbolize so much about menopause?

The Many Facets of Menopause

I have shared my new perspective on Snow White and her seven little friends with women who are at midlife and beyond who I encounter in my practice as a health care professional (I'm both a nurse and a naturopathic doctor) as well as among my circle of friends and have found that there hasn't been one who couldn't identify with most, if not all of the characters. Vague new symptoms, fatigue, irritability, foggy minds, feeling confident and up one day and crashing with doubt and depression the next. And as if these weren't challenging enough to deal with, there is the confusion as to what we're supposed to do to manage the roller-coaster ride of our fluctuating hormones. Should we take hormones and if so, how long and what type? How much of what specific nutritional supplements do we need to take to address all the symptoms? What amounts of estrogen and progesterone should we take? Do we need to be concerned with other declining hormones in our bodies?

Menopause is a complex, multifaceted process. Although much of the focus of menopause centers on managing hormonal changes, that is only one piece of the whole puzzle. Equally and perhaps more important are issues such as engaging in positive health practices and etching out purposeful, powerful lives for the second half of our adult years.

From a societal and spiritual perspective (I'm a Christian who believes in the wisdom of the Bible) I see no evidence that menopause is supposed to mark the end of our lives as active contributors to society, grant us permission to self-indulge now that family responsibilities are lessened, or allow us to become self-absorbed in our own problems to the exclusion of those in the world external to ourselves. Quite the contrary. The relief from the demands of raising a young family and the wisdom and experiences gained from decades of living can equip women to make profound contributions. Menopause can mark the beginning of a new and dynamic season of our lives.

Midlife Transition

There is no magic age when one enters midlife. Rather, midlife is a time of new awareness. Small print is unreadable without glasses. Rich foods that had been enjoyed without thought in the past now result in heartburn and extra weight on the hips. Hair on the head grays and thins while thick, dark facial hairs threaten to form a moustache if not regularly plucked. Skin sags, dries, and wrinkles. Activities are planned strategically to accommodate changing energy levels. Napping is antici-pated with more enthusiasm than having sex.

In addition to visible physical signs, there are other indicators of midlife. Children are becoming more independent and needing you less. The parents who had provided help to you throughout the years now in-creasingly need your assistance. The death of people you know becomes common enough that obituaries become regular reading.

If you're working you begin noticing that you are among the more senior employees; you begin to think about retirement and investigate the amount to expect in your Social Security check. If you've been a full-time homemaker you begin getting a little antsy with fewer responsibilities and wonder if you should try to find a job or a new hobby. Little voices calling you Granny or Nanna, sweet as they may be, cause you to question the ap-propriateness of blasting Rolling Stones music when you're driving alone and wearing sexy underwear.

Midlife attacks like an infestation of fleas: unwelcomed, unexpect-ed, and unable to ignore.

Controlling the symptoms associated with menopause is impor-tant, but only part of what you need to be concerned with at this stage of life. Menopause occurs at about the same time that many of the effects of aging begin to be acutely noticed. These effects are both a reflection of some of the common changes that the body experiences after decades of use and the consequences of the care you took of your body. You can compare this to a house. Over the years, even the best of structures will experience some degree of faded paint, cracks in the plaster, and breakdown of plumb-ing. If the owners have been attentive to protecting the structure and tak-ing care of problems promptly, their house can continue to be attractive and functional for a long time. However, if they abused the house by neglect-ing to paint exposed wood, driving large nails into cracking plaster, and ignoring the leaks which continuously dripped water on the floor, the life, function, and appearance of their property will decline rapidly. Likewise, although all bodies will experience some changes with the wear and tear of aging, vast differences among people of the same age can result from life-style practices that affect health.

If you've been among the individuals who have been conscientious with their health habits, congratulations and keep up the good work. However, if you've been less than perfect, menopause can be the time when you commit to charting a new course. You're still at an age when you can reverse many of the consequences of poor habits and not only add more years to your life, but more life to your remaining years.

For our mothers' and grandmothers' generations, when life expectancy was barely age 60, there was little need to consider making changes in the 4th, 5th, or 6th decades of life to obtain future gains. However, today's women in the U.S. enjoy a life expectancy of over 80 years, with the potential to live well into their 90s. If you were to list the life experiences you've had in the past three decades (e.g., children graduating or marrying, welcoming new grandchildren, career changes, moving to a new home, acquiring a disease, losing and gaining friends, etc.) the list may be quite long. Is there any reason to think that you won't have an equally long list developed during the next three decades?

Women at midlife and beyond have considerable life remaining. The ability to live those years fully, anticipate each day with enthusiasm, and be a blessing rather than burden to others largely depends on your health. Fortunately, there is much you can do to influence your health status.

Building Blocks for Health

You are a complex creation comprised of body, mind, and spirit. These various facets of you are inseparable; balance and harmony among them are essential for health. In the holistic circles in which I travel I come in contact with many people who are highly health-conscious by secular standards. They eat nutritious diets, keep firm muscles by exercising regularly, build stress-relieving practices into their lifestyles, and keep abreast of the latest health-promoting alternative therapies. However, many have no faith or spiritual foundation and feed their spiritual hunger by flocking to hear the latest in-vogue "mystics", seeking guidance from crystals and tarot cards, communicating with vague "spirits", or venturing to exotic places to meditate with spiritual guides. Without a strong spiritual foundation, these individuals are not whole---healthy--- regardless of how great they look or feel.

On the other hand, strong faith will not guarantee health. I also have come in contact with a fair number of Christians who pray, attend church, serve in ministries, and are committed to a close relationship with the Lord. However, some of these people are grossly overweight, have lifestyles that guarantee high levels of stress, or are so involved with their ministries that they have little time left for exercise, solitude, or quality relationships. They miss the mark, as well. Belief in God doesn't mean you can neglect or abuse your body and mind; in fact, this is dishonoring to Him. There must be concern for the whole---body, mind, and spirit.

It is important to understand that *health is about balance---not perfection.* You needn't look like a model, possess the mental prowess of a rocket scientist, or engage in prayer all of your waking hours to be healthy. But, you do need to respect and care for your total being---body, mind, and spirit--- so that you can be whole.

The journey to wholeness is not without sacrifice and challenges. And, it doesn't mean that you will be free from aches, pains, and diseases. Health---wholeness---is possible in the presence of adversity, imperfection, and illness when you view these obstacles as purposeful challenges and opportunities for growth.

A Holistic Approach is Needed

Changes experienced at midlife impact every aspect of a woman's life--body, mind, and spirit. Among the challenges faced, the major ones are to:

- manage distressing and disruptive symptoms caused by hormonal changes
- strengthen and/or develop positive lifestyle practices that promote good health
- use talents, gifts, experience, and wisdom to realize one's purpose

These challenges demand an individualized holistic approach to navigating the specific issues that are faced.

A holistic approach recognizes that the various aspects of an individual---physical, mental, and spiritual---are interwoven and indivisible, and profoundly affect each other. In the context of health, a holistic approach refers to the integration of the mind, body, and spirit to create a dynamic whole that is more powerful and significant than the individual components would suggest. The synergy can yield surprisingly profound results. For instance, managing the physical symptoms of menopause alone may improve a woman's life by 30%; addressing physical health in totality, gaining insight into emotional issues that impact her well-being, and reducing barriers to a full spiritual life could improve her life by 100% or better. 1+1+1 = 5 or 10 or more. This is what holistic health is all about.

Although the term holistic health gained popularity in the last quarter of the 20th Century, the relationship of body, mind, and spirit was revealed from the earliest of times. Solomon declared that *a cheerful heart is good medicine but a crushed spirit dries up the bones* (Proverbs 17:22) acknowledging that our mood impacts our physical body. Jesus Christ interacted with people holistically. One example in which this was shown is the story of the woman who had suffered with hemorrhaging for twelve years and was healed by touching Jesus' garments (Mark 5:25-34). Jesus told her that her faith had made her well, offering the message that our spiritual state in being faithful to Him was of utmost importance and could affect one's physical condition. Buddha affirmed that the mind affects all parts of one's being when he said that "the mind is everything. What you think you become". Today numerous holistic practitioners, alternative therapists, and growing numbers of traditional health care providers support that health depends on the status of all facets of a person.

Becoming Women Afire

Women Afire is the term we'll be using to offer a different perspective on women at midlife and beyond. By living a purposeful life a woman can help to shift the view of women at this season of life from that of over-the-hill beings who need to move out of the way for the young to that of dynamic examples of purposeful, passionate lives. Implicit in this is taking care of her body, mind, and spirit. Later in the book we'll be reviewing some of the essentials of health care practices that enable a woman to do that.

I'd like to suggest that Women Afire be leaders in casting a new vision for women at midlife and beyond to one which unleashes the power and honors the beauty of this season of life. It can be very difficult to be a middle-aged or elder woman in our youth-oriented society. Clothes are made to display youthful, firm bodies. Unless they are hawking household items or laxatives, few mature women are seen in advertisements. Rather than be concerned for what it says about their ability to appreciate the below-the-surface depth and life experiences of a partner of equal age, many people envy men with young trophy wives. In the workplace, youth often substitutes for experience in providing a competitive advantage.

Unfortunately, it is not only men and young people who are responsible for perpetuating the value that young is better in women: aging women do it to themselves. We plunk down mega-bucks for age-defying potions and make-up artistry. We subject ourselves to tucks, lifts, and suctions. When celebrities of our generation surgically maintain the same appearance they had in their 20s, we often admire rather than question their reluctance to accept that 50 or 60 or 70 years olds are supposed to have a few more wrinkles and lines than their grandchildren.

Now let me state clearly, I am not suggesting that women not try to look their best and be in optimal shape. Nothing is wrong with cosmetics, flattering hairstyles, and attractive clothing. To my knowledge, there is no commandment that states thou shall look dowdy. Likewise, exercising to keep muscles toned, bones strong, cardiovascular function optimal, and energy high is a sensible health practice that shows good stewardship for the bodies we've been given. It is when women invest an inordinate amount of time, money, or energy on their appearance, feel that they must subject themselves to unnecessary procedures to eliminate signs of aging, or hate what they see in the mirror that they cross the line from wanting to present their best image to denying or despising the reality of their God-created being---wrinkles, lines, and all.

Women Afire can demonstrate to the world that there is something that sets them apart. They can show that they are valued not because they look like Barbie Dolls, but because of the meaningful contributions they continue to make---just as they are. Perhaps a valuable movement of Women Afire can unfold that demonstrates a new way of *being* for women at midlife and beyond... one in which societal pressures to deny aging and promote an artificial young appearance are loudly rejected and decades of accumulated experiences, wisdom, and giftedness are unleashed to make a difference in this world. By realizing themselves as called to make a difference, Women Afire could redefine the aging experience for their sisters and lead them to a vibrant life.

Roadmap for Your Journey to Health and Wholeness

When you're taking a trip by car, you probably start by determining your destination. For example, you may plan to travel from Maine to Florida. Along the way, you want to catch a ball game at Fenway Park, take some photos of the Statue of Liberty, visit Aunt Ethel in Philadelphia, grab a crab cake dinner at Baltimore's Harborplace, swing by Charleston to do some antiquing, and ultimately arrive in Disney World. You have a general idea of the location of these various destinations but chances are, you wouldn't jump in your car and start driving without a roadmap that could direct you to the best routes.

Your journey to health and wholeness is no different. In order to reach the goals of controlling perimenopausal and menopausal symptoms, achieving optimal health, and realizing your purpose, you need to understand the factors that can lead you to these destinations. This may require you to gather facts, hone your skills, confront obstacles that could detour your plans, experience things you hadn't intended, and invest more time and energy than expected. Thinking that you can change the way you feel and act with an effortless quick fix is about as realistic as believing you can accomplish your Maine to Florida travel plans in a single day.

This book will serve as a roadmap to assist you on your journey. It will help you to:

- understand the realities of perimenopause and menopause
- identify factors that influence your ability to have a healthy, abundant life
- evaluate your current health status
- learn strategies for promoting health
- achieve a balanced life through the practice of spiritual disciplines
- experience the fullness of a purposeful, powerful life

Helpful information can be gained by merely sitting back and reading the content of this book. However, you'll get the most from this book by being an active participant. Grab a pen and some paper, jot down your reactions, answer the questions, and complete the exercises that you'll find. Answer the study questions; better yet, partner with some friends and discuss them together. Get ready to equip yourself to be a Woman Afire!

CHAPTER 1

Feeding Your Body Wisely

You can't help getting older, but
you don't have to grow old.
~George Burns~

As dry as it may seem to address a topic like sensible eating habits this early in the book, your diet has profound effects on every aspect of your health. Further, food concerns—obtaining, preparing, consuming—do absorb some of our attention each day. It seems that half the population is talking about the latest diet craze and the other half about the newest restaurant or recipe they've found. Food is a hot topic of interest and certainly has more significance than merely providing nourishment for the body. Learning the significance of food to you is a good starting point in building good dietary practices as this can help you to identify patterns that may need to be changed.

1

My own eating habits can demonstrate some of the challenges in adhering to good dietary practices. Like many people, when I'm traveling and eating in restaurants, my diet tends to include many items that I wouldn't regularly eat at home. This posed no major problem for me until my work caused me to travel frequently. As I hurried from one terminal to another to meet a tight plane connection it was easier to grab a double-dipped ice cream cone that I could eat on the run than to find and consume something more nutritious. When I finally arrived at the hotel, tired and stressed, a bacon cheeseburger (usually a quarter-pounder) and fries were much more comforting than a broiled chicken breast and broccoli. And of course, when local acquaintances asked me to accompany them to the best restaurants in the area, I *had* to sample the special delicacies that had a tendency to be high in fat and calories. If this had happened once in awhile it would have been manageable, but when I was out of town weekly, my exceptions to a nutritious diet were becoming routine. Something had to change. I now try to pack nutritious snacks in my carry-on bag so that I can avoid fast food pick-me-ups and discipline myself to select from restaurants' lower fat menu items. Do I ever slip? You bet! But straying from the path of good eating even one-third of the time still beats the unhealthy food consumption that was typical for me nearly every time I ate out while away from home in the past.

What influences your eating? Do you look to food as a means of comfort and relaxation like I did when I was traveling? Is eating a source of entertainment or a means of showing and receiving love? Is your schedule so hectic that you commonly dine on fast foods? Do you follow strict dietary practices to prevent or manage a health condition? Are you among the small minority who gives minimal attention to eating and consumes only enough to survive?

After you do some honest self-evaluation and identify behaviors that you need to change, your next step is to make sure you consume a nutritious diet. Your body needs proper nourishment to function normally, repair damaged tissue, reproduce cells, protect itself from infection and disease, and have ample energy to participate in the usual activities of daily living. Good nutrition means that the quality and quantity of your food intake is adequate to meet your body's needs. Excesses or deficiencies in nutrients can contribute to poor health.

Nutrition facts aren't exactly the type of material that make for interesting bedtime reading, yet it's important to have a basic understanding of them to make sensible, healthy choices. With that in mind, read through the next few pages to get a crash course on nutrients. Try to get a general understanding of the main points and return to this section in the future when you have specific questions.

Nutrition Facts

The various nutrients needed to keep the body in balance can be categorized by *macronutrients* and *micronutrients*. Macronutrients consist of:

- *Carbohydrates* that are the main source of energy for the body and help with digestion and metabolism of proteins and fats. They can take the form of simple carbohydrates that come from sources like table sugars and fruits, or complex carbohydrates that are provided by foods like potatoes, rice, and cereals. A high intake of complex carbohydrates and a low intake of simple carbohydrates are recommended. As carbohydrates can be major contributors to the weight gain that you may experience during menopause, you want to watch this category carefully. Make wise selections, such as multigrain toast over a Danish.

- *Proteins* that build, repair, and maintain body tissue, produce antibodies, regulate the body's acid-base balance, and detoxify harmful substances. Proteins are large complex molecules made of amino acids that each have a specific function. A complete protein contains all of the amino acids; meat and dairy products are examples of complete proteins. Nuts, grains, and legumes are examples of incomplete proteins; they must be combined in certain ways or with a complete protein to provide a balanced amount of amino acids. It's a good idea to consume a protein with every meal.

- *Fats* that are concentrated forms of heat and energy. Different classifications of fats have different functions, such as to help to synthesize essential compounds in the body and control body temperature. Sources of fats are whole-milk products, meats, eggs, nuts, peanut butter, olives, avocados, and vegetable oils.

Attached to macronutrients are micronutrients which consist of *vitamins* and *minerals*. Vitamins aid in metabolism and in releasing energy from digested food. Along with enzymes, vitamins act as catalysts in chemical reactions within the body. Minerals help in the formation and maintenance of body fluids, blood, bone, and the nervous system. A description of common vitamins and minerals is offered in Table 1 in the Appendix..

All nutrients are important to your body, but it is important to assure the right balance of their consumption. A healthy diet is rich in grains, fruits, and vegetables and limited in fats and refined and processed sugars and starches. The MyPlate icon shown in Figure 1 is a simple visual that shows the recommended amount of various nutrients that should be consumed on a daily basis.

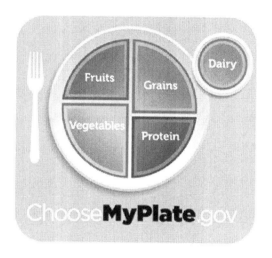

Fluid intake

Good fluid intake is essential to health. If you did nothing but lay still all day, your body would still lose 64-80 ounces of water through fluids lost through breathing, perspiring, voiding, and bowel elimination. If you live in a dry environment or have an active lifestyle, your fluid loss is greater. To maintain fluid balance you need to consume at least the amount of fluids that your body loses, which for the average individual is six to eight 8-ounce glasses of fluids daily. A helpful way to determine your fluid requirements is to drink one-half of your body weight in ounces each day.

For example, if a woman weighs 130 pounds, half of that number is 65, so she would try to consume at least 65 ounces of fluids daily, or a little more than eight 8 ounce glasses or cups. Most of your fluid intake should be in the form of plain water. While coffee, tea, sodas, and alcoholic beverages do contain water, they also contain substances that can increase fluid loss and could threaten your body's health, so limit their intake. (You may find it helpful to brew a quart of decaffeinated green tea each day to keep in your refrigerator and consume throughout the day. In addition to assuring that you're getting at least half your daily fluid requirements, you'll get the health benefits from this wonderful brew.)

Eating habits

It is important to establish eating habits that support the principles of good nutrition. There is a risk that if you skip a meal you'll go for the candy bar or chips when you begin to feel hunger pangs, so schedule meals. (Later, you'll be asked to review your typical food intake when you complete your self-assessment which can help you to spot bad habits.)

Breakfast is important. You don't need to consume a large breakfast, just a smart one. Rather than coffee and a sweet bun, eat some fresh fruit, grain cereal with skim milk or yogurt, and juice. After breakfast you may want to take a good multivitamin supplement. Although the statement is made that "if you eat right you don't need a supplement", the reality is that most of us do not eat right. It can be quite challenging to consume the proper quantity and quality of food to obtain the recommended daily allowance of most nutrients. Few of us have the benefit of eating freshly picked fruits and vegetables; the longer the period between when these items were picked and when they reach your table, the greater the loss of nutrients. Further, the processing and cooking of food causes some vitamins and minerals to be lost. A daily multivitamin supplement can compensate for these factors and assure you get the basic micronutrients that you need.

Although a single daily multivitamin supplement can be beneficial, don't overdo a good thing. *Megavitamin therapy*---also called orthomolecular therapy---has become popular in some circles. This involves taking high doses of vitamins, minerals, and amino acids. There are claims that megavitamin therapy can help a wide range of health conditions, such as attention deficit disorder, schizophrenia, and allergies, however, research is inconclusive at this time. In addition to ingesting costly supplements that you don't need, using high doses of vitamins and minerals can be dangerous. For example, large doses of vitamin E can thin the blood and cause bleeding; excess vitamin D can increase the blood pressure and cause muscle and bone pain; high intakes of vitamin A can cause anemia and joint pain. Avoid megavitamin therapy unless you are under the direction of a health care professional.

Be sure to buy your supplements from reputable sources and to check the expiration dates. Read the labels carefully as one manufacturer's product may require 3 tablets to consume the same doses that you could obtain from one tablet of another product---which can be a considerable factor in cost! Unfortunately, the quality of supplements can vary from distributor to distributor, and a higher cost doesn't assure a higher quality. If you seriously want to research the quality of supplements produced by various companies you may want to visit the website of ConsumerLab.com, a company that conducts independent product reviews. (General information is free; a nominal fee is charged to be a subscriber and have access to a wider range of information and services.)

In addition to the *what* of your eating habits, also consider the *how*. Do you gulp food down without giving your taste buds a chance to detect what is passing through? Are you mindlessly shoving food in your mouth while you're plastered in front of the television set? Have you created your version of Meals on Wheels by hastily eating while negotiating rush hour traffic with a carload of kids? Enjoying the dining *experience* is an important aspect of eating wisely. You needn't set the table with your finest china, and serve elaborate meals every day to enjoy the dining experience, but little niceties can make a difference.

My husband and I know a wonderful couple who demonstrate this point. Kathy and Rick work full time and have busy schedules, yet they've committed that barring unusual circumstances, their dinners at home will be by candlelight. They may be eating leftovers or carryout foods, but they do it by candlelight with the lights dimmed. This relatively minor touch creates an atmosphere that allows them to transition from their busy-ness to calmness. I wonder how many ordinary mealtimes could become dining experiences with minor environmental modifications like candles or soft music.

Eating also can become a dining experience by taking the time to enjoy what you're eating. Try experimenting for a day in making a conscious effort to identify all the sensations of all the food you eat: the crunching sound as you bite into an apple, the aroma of coffee, the smooth surface of a tomato, the ridges of a raisin as you roll it on your tongue, the different flavors and colors of the food you encounter in one meal. Our creator certainly could have made a single food substance to fulfill our nutritional needs, however, He chose to bless us with a wide range of flavors, colors, textures, scents, and even sounds to stimulate our senses and offer greater pleasure to us as we eat. To take the time to enjoy food is one way to show appreciation for this blessing---and to derive greater health benefits from eating.

Weight control

An adult with a body mass index (BMI) between 25 and 29.9 is considered overweight and one with a BMI of 30 or higher is considered obese. Approximately 33% of American adults are overweight and another 35% are obese.

To Calculate Your Body Mass Index (BMI)

Divide your weight in pounds by your height in inches squared.

Then take that number and multiply it by 703.

Round to the second decimal place.

Example: Weight = 150 lbs, Height = 5'5" (65")

Calculation: [150 ÷ (65)²] x 703 > [150 ÷ 4225] x 703 > 0.035 x 703 = 24.96

(If you're not great at math, there are BMI calculators on the internet that you can just plug your weight and height into that will do the calculations for you.)

Although genetic factors, some medications (e.g., steroids, tricyclic antidepressants, antihypertensives), and a few diseases can cause some people to become obese, the reason most people gain weight is because their caloric input exceeds their caloric expenditure. A sedentary lifestyle and high-fat, high-carbohydrate diet are significant risk factors for obesity.

Some people have been obese for most of their lives even in the absence of genetic factors, disease, and drug effects. This frequently is related to the role of food and eating in their families. My own background exemplifies this. I am from a Greek family and was raised in a Greek community. If you've ever known Greeks, visited Greece, or seen the movie *My Big Fat Greek Wedding,* you probably understand that the Greeks have some fantastic foods and they love to eat. In my childhood home, my stay-at-home mom prepared fine meals just about every day. (In fact, I can remember as a kid begging my mother to please stop serving us mousaka, spinach pie, souvlaki, and all that other "awful Greek stuff" and give us some all-American hot dogs, burgers, and canned spaghetti.) You can believe that after spending hours preparing those wonderful dishes, my mother wanted to see the fruits of her labor consumed, so there was considerable pressure put on my brother and me to eat. Neither he nor I had particularly large appetites (thankfully!) so dinner table battles were frequent as our parents urged us to eat against our resistance. To make matters worse, every social encounter involved food---and not just light snacks but a fully loaded table with Greek meatballs, feta cheese, loaves of crusty bread, olives, baklava, and on and on and on. To enter a Greek home and not sample the food that was offered was considered a major insult. When most of your family and social acquaintances are Greek this means life nearly becomes a moveable feast. A reasonable appetite and high energy level enabled me to escape becoming obese; however, I have relatives and friends who were less fortunate and are living with the consequences.

Your beliefs and practices about eating that you developed from your family also may have been built on erroneous information. My husband describes an ongoing battle at his childhood dinner table---where potatoes were served daily---between his father and brother. His brother wanted to eat generous portions of green vegetables and skip the potatoes. His dad believed you needed the heartiness of potatoes rather than "those green vegetables that wouldn't do you any good or put meat on your bones", and scolded the boy for not consuming his daily pile of the starchy vegetable. Be it the misinformation gained about the nutritional value of certain foods, unhealthy cooking methods, or unsound eating habits, the foundation our families laid strongly influences our lifelong eating habits and can be a significant factor in obesity.

Another contributing factor to obesity is that food may be meeting other needs in your life. For example, you may lack purpose, love, or relationships in your life and fulfill these emotional needs by seeking the comfort of food (and usually not the carrots and celery variety!). I once led a weight control group for women in a community health program. Many of these women were middle-aged homemakers who no longer had children at home and who shared little interests with their husbands. They spent many hours alone in their homes while their husbands where gone, working, bowling, and socializing with the guys at the local tavern. For the most part, they passed their time watching television and snacking as they did. Thus began the unfortunate cycle:

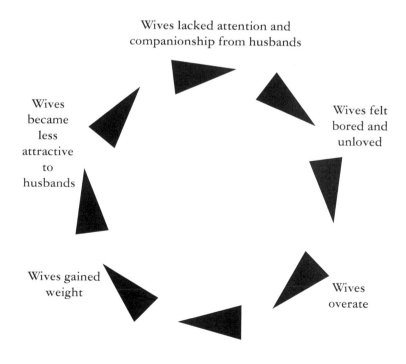

Wives lacked attention and companionship from husbands

Wives felt bored and unloved

Wives overate

Wives gained weight

Wives became less attractive to husbands

Food was used by these women to numb the pain of unsatisfying marriages and boredom. Although education and guidance in dietary modifications were offered to this group, the more significant ways that I impacted their weight loss were to guide them in exploring their emotional reasons for eating, encourage them to become involved in activities outside the home, and help them learn ways to express their needs and communicate more effectively with their husbands.

In that same weight control group another issue arose which can influence the ability to lose weight: lack of family support for the goal of weight loss. There was a woman in the group whose situation reflected this. Irma, who barely stood five feet tall, weighed 225 pounds. She shared that she had weighed about 110 pounds when she had married 19 years ago and progressively gained weight until she reached her current level of obesity. Irma's beautiful features made it easy to imagine that she must have turned quite a few heads back then. Initially, Irma was showing a weight loss at her weekly weigh-ins but about six weeks into the program, she hit a plateau and then began gaining weight again. At first, Irma pretended to have no idea why this was happening, but then confessed that she had been "slipping". In exploring this with Irma, I learned that just when people started to notice that she was losing weight, her husband began bringing home fattening goodies on a daily basis. The longstanding problem of weak willpower compounded by strong urging by her husband to "go ahead and have some; I bought this just for you!" caused her to succumb to temptation. With the group's support, Irma armed herself to try to get on track and asked her husband to avoid bringing home any edible treats. Although her husband ignored her request, the group's support helped her to follow her diet and she again began to shed the pounds. I then received a telephone call from Irma informing me that her husband was making her drop out of the group. "He told me he likes me just the way I am and that I

12

don't have to lose any weight." Further into the conversation Irma revealed that her husband had hinted that if she got thin, she may no longer be satisfied with him or may want to return to work rather than be at home for him. His insecurities caused him to sabotage her diet efforts. Obviously, the understanding and support of one's family are key ingredients to successfully changing eating habits.

If obesity is an issue with you, reflect on your beliefs about food, cultural influences, family dynamics, relationships, and emotional needs that influence your overeating. Pray for insights and direction. List the factors you've identified and write some realistic steps you can take to change them. You may find it beneficial to recruit a friend to assist you with this process.

Before starting to diet, get a complete physical examination. In addition to learning about any special precautions you need to heed while dieting based on your unique health status, an examination can unveil health conditions that are contributing to your weight gain, such as endocrine disturbances or a tumor.

Avoid extreme diets or weight loss fads as these are difficult to sustain on a long-term basis and could pose serious health risks. The goal is not to take off as much weight as possible as quickly as you can, but to make lifestyle modifications that can help to improve your overall health and maintain your weight within a healthy range. Some principles to guide you are offered on the pages that follow.

Tips for Weight Reduction

- Consult with your health care practitioner to determine if there are any factors you must consider as you begin a weight reduction program.
- Review your beliefs, attitudes, and experiences that contribute to unhealthy eating habits. Reflect on the reasons you overeat.
- Elicit your family's support.
- Keep a food diary for several days prior to starting your diet. Examine it for factors that contribute to obesity, such as skipping a meal and then binging on sweets, consuming a disproportionate amount of fats.
- Determine your desired calorie intake and plot how this will be divided over the day.
- Follow a sensible eating plan. Avoid starvation diets, fads, or over-the-counter medications.
- Consume a balanced diet that includes at least 100 gram of carbohydrates and 50 to 100 grams of protein (predominately from foods that are low in saturated fat and cholesterol).
- Take a daily multivitamin supplement.
- Avoid high-protein diets. Although they can cause initial weight loss and reduce appetite because the high fat content satisfies you, high protein diets can increase your risk for cardiovascular disease, osteoporosis, and perhaps cancer. The extra excretion of body fluids caused by these diets also increases the workload of your kidneys.
- Consume foods with a low *glycemic index*. The glycemic index ranks foods by how they affect blood sugar. Foods with a low glycemic index break down slowly, and consequently, release their energy at a

slower rate which in turn, helps you feel fuller longer. These foods also help to keep the blood sugar stable which prevents you from feeling hungry. Foods with a low glycemic index include foods such as whole grain breads, pumpernickel, all bran cereal, toasted muesli, yogurt, milk, apples, oranges, peaches, lentils, soybeans, and baked beans.

- Begin each day with a prayer for strength and discipline to adhere to your dietary plan.
- Start or increase your current exercise program to increase your metabolic rate. In addition, take advantage of opportunities in your daily routine to boost your activity level (e.g., walking stairs instead of taking an elevator, parking at the farthest space on the lot).
- Drink at least 8 glasses of water throughout the day. If it is difficult for you to drink that much plain water, try drinking flavored seltzer water or decaffeinated herbal teas. (A cup of peppermint tea taken before meals can help in reducing appetite.)
- Keep plenty of celery and carrots on hand to munch on between meals.
- If you slip off your diet, don't be too hard on yourself. Changing any habit is difficult. Explore the reasons for straying from your plan and try to address them, including specifically praying for strength to avoid having them interfere with your goal again.
- Rejoice in your progress.

Fasting

The chemicals that are consumed in the average American diet cause toxins to accumulate in the body that can lead to a variety of ill effects. One method to eliminate these toxins is by fasting. Fasting has been used since the earliest of times to cleanse the body and sharpen the spirit. The Bible shows that more than 800 years before the birth of Jesus Christ, Jesoshaphat called upon the people of Judah to fast so that they could seriously focus on their sin and pray for God's help (2 Chronicles 20:3-4). When returning to Jerusalem, Ezra and his co-travelers fasted and prayed to seek the spiritual preparation for their journey (Ezra 8:23). Jesus fasted for 40 days and nights in the desert (Matthew 4:2) and emphasized the right reasons to fast: to spend time in prayer and reflect on God's blessings (Matthew 6:16-18). Jesus urged those who fasted to *"not look somber"* or *"disfigure their faces to show men they are fasting"* but to look and act as normally as possible. This remains solid advice to follow in your fasting. By going about business as usual and not drawing attention to your fast, you will be less likely to be preoccupied with symptoms and can ease your burden. Fasting teaches self-discipline and offers the opportunity to turn your thoughts to higher level issues. (If you do nothing more than use the time you would have spent in purchasing, preparing, and eating food in meditation or prayer you have done well!)

There are various types of fasts that you can do ranging from the ingestion of nothing but water, to consuming only juices and fruits. Fasting can last anywhere from one day to several weeks. If you are healthy and there is no medical problem that would be affected by fasting, you should experience no difficulty with a two-day fast consisting of only water intake or a five-day fast in which only water and juices are ingested. Prolonged fasts or fasts in the presence of health conditions need to be conducted under the supervision of a health professional. Fasting usually is not advised for persons with diabetes, hypoglycemia, eating disorders, malnutrition, cancer, infectious diseases, renal or liver disease, ulcerative colitis, or bronchial asthma; women who are pregnant should not fast.

Fasting stimulates a cleansing and removal of toxins from the body which can cause some physical effects, including:

- coated tongue
- unpleasant taste
- halitosis
- increased body odor
- skin dryness
- headache
- fatigue
- dizziness
- insomnia
- nausea
- aching joints
- flu-like symptoms
- reduced pulse and blood pressure.

In some persons, an irregular heartbeat can occur. A several pound weight loss is common.

You don't need to drastically modify your activities for short-term fasts, although it is best to avoid strenuous exercise. You may want to schedule extra rest periods on the days when you fast. A good fluid intake during the fast is essential.

Good personal hygiene is important while fasting. As toxins are eliminated through the skin, frequent bathing is useful, including gently scrubbing of the skin with a soft brush. Frequent oral hygiene is needed, as well. (Rinsing the mouth with lemon juice can reduce tongue coating and unpleasant tastes. Be sure to follow this with a rinse with water to protect your teeth's enamel from the acidic effects of the lemon juice.)

There is some belief that the elimination of toxins and other beneficial effects of fasting can be accomplished in a gentler way with a *cleansing diet* such as:

Breakfast: low-sugar fruit eaten whole

One hour before lunch: water

Lunch: steamed vegetables and a grain product

One hour before supper: fresh vegetable juice

Supper: soup (noncream) or salad

This low-fat, high-fiber vegetarian diet provides a continuous cleansing effect without the stress of a fast.

Fasting is a spiritual discipline, therefore spiritual preparation accompanies physical preparation for a fast. Prior to fasting, pray for guidance for the type of fast you need. While fasting, think about the attributes of God and the ways in which He has blessed your life. Be open to the voice of the Spirit. Expect spiritual opposition as your bodily symptoms challenge you to forfeit your fast; pray for help as you resist the temptation to prematurely break your fast. Discipline your mind to focus on your desire for spiritual growth rather than your sacrifice of food, remembering that: *Blessed are those who hunger and thirst for righteousness for they will be filled* (Matthew 5:6).

And What Goes In Does Come Out

Despite not ranking at the top of the list of popular topics of social conversation, eliminating wastes from the body is crucial to health. Wastes from your tissues are carried in the blood to the kidneys where they are filtered and excreted in urine. A good fluid intake assists in removing these waste products.

Bowel elimination tends to be a greater problem for most people than urinary elimination, evidenced by laxative sales in this country. Often, irregularity in bowel elimination is the result of diet or inactivity. The hormonal changes experienced at menopause can contribute to constipation, also. In addition to some exercise, bowel elimination can be promoted by:

- Eating a high-fiber diet, including foods such as fruits, vegetables, nuts, seeds, beans, and whole unrefined grains
- Reducing the consumption of processed foods
- Drinking several glasses of juice daily
- Providing adequate time for toileting

If constipation is a problem, natural measures rather than medications can be used as a first line of attack to help stimulate bowel movements. A daily tablespoon of psyllium husks, wheat bran, or flaxseed meal can prove useful; be sure to drink plenty of fluids when you use these. Vitamin C supplements (not to exceed 5000 mg per day) can help to soften stools, and herbs like dandelion root, cascara sagrada, senna, and rhubarb can be used for their laxative effect.

You need only examine the labels of popular foods to see that a variety of chemicals are ingested through the average American diet. These chemicals can cause toxins to accumulate in the body and threaten your health. Elimination of these toxins is helpful and fasting is a beneficial means of accomplishing this. You may want to plan an occasional fast, such as one day each month.

Don't be hard on yourself if your eating habits have been less than ideal. Few people consistently eat a perfect diet and, unfortunately, many of the foods that are not good for our health frequently tempt us because they tend to taste great. If you need to makes changes make them realistic for you. And, if you happen to go off track with an occasional splurge, avoid getting discouraged and giving up. Small steps to progress are better than no progress at all.

Study Questions

1. Reflect on your childhood and identify the messages that were conveyed about eating.
2. What factors cause you to eat in an unhealthy manner?
3. How do your emotions affect your eating?
4. What would be your greatest challenges to changing your eating patterns? How could you overcome them?

CHAPTER 2

Balancing Activity and Rest

Exercise and application produce order in our affairs, health of body,
cheerfulness of mind, and these make us precious to our friends.
~Thomas Jefferson~

Movement involves changing from one position or place to another. Your internal body is in a constant state of motion, witnessed by the circulation of blood through your vessels, the exchange of air in your lungs, the passage of food through your digestive tract, and the blinking of your eyes. Some of the movements you make, such as walking, are the result of voluntary effort on your part. Others, such as the secretion of hormones and the filtration of wastes through the kidneys, occur without you consciously having to think about them. Our maker's creative capacity certainly is evidenced in these purposeful, efficient, and complex activities of the human body.

Movement and exercise of the body have numerous benefits, particularly for women at menopause and beyond. You will need to tailor an exercise program to your individual needs. Before embarking on any exercise program, be sure to have a physical examination so that you'll be aware of any precautions you must heed. For instance, some heart and blood pressure medications can alter your heart's response to exercise, demanding that some adjustments be made. (Specific guidelines regarding exercise will be offered later.)

BENEFITS OF EXERCISE

- Improves circulation
- Strengthens immune system
- Aids in reducing weight and body fat
- Increases bone density and strength
- Keeps muscles strong and in tone
- Reduces blood pressure
- Increases lung capacity and air exchange
- Increases insulin sensitivity and glucose tolerance
- Promotes regular bowel elimination
- Reduces risk of some cancers
- Elevates mood
- Increases energy
- Improves mental function
- Promotes restful sleep
- Relieves stress

Like many women, you may believe that you are getting ample exercise because you are on the go throughout the day. Actually, you can be physically active to the point of exhaustion but not truly exercising. Exercise is the conscious act of moving in order to maintain strength or function. There are different types of exercises, including:

- *Flexibility:* gentle stretching, such as tai chi or yoga, that are useful to do daily
- *Strengthening:* exercises that should be done every other day to develop and improve muscle tone, such as weight training, playing tennis, and performing physical labor
- *Aerobic:* exercises that involve activities such as brisk walking, bicycling, jumping rope, and swimming that are helpful to do at least several times during the week

Consider the amount of exercise you get in a typical day. If you're not doing so at present, try to schedule some regular form of exercise (e.g., walking, playing ball, an aerobics class) at least several times during the week---or, ideally, daily. If you're unaccustomed to exercising start with a 10 minutes session and then progress to 20 minutes as your tolerance and condition improve. In addition, take advantage of opportunities to increase your exercise during your routine day; this could include:

- walking stairs instead of taking elevators
- parking in the farthest spot from the building
- using part of your lunch time to take a short walk
- taking a few minutes each hour to stretch and bend

When doing exercises for cardiopulmonary endurance---such as jogging, walking, cycling, swimming, and other forms of aerobic exercises---it is beneficial to *determine your heart rate during exercise* to assure that the rate stays within a safe range. To do this, subtract your age from the figure 220 to obtain your *maximum heart rate* and multiply that answer by 70% (0.7) to obtain your *target heart rate.*

220

-____   *Your age*

       Maximum heart rate

x 0.7

       Target heart rate

Your heart rate should stay in a range of 10 beats of your target heart rate during exercise. For example, if you are 45 years of age, your heart rate should fall within 112 and 133 beats per minute based on the following calculation:

220

- 45

175   *Maximum heart rate*

x 0.7

122.5 *Target heart rate*

If your heart rate during exercise is more than 10 beats above the target heart rate the exercise should be reduced the next time it is done. If your heart rate is more than 10 beats lower than the target heart rate, you should increase the intensity of your exercise the next time to assure you are obtaining the best cardiopulmonary benefit. (Heart rate monitors can be used as alternatives to manually taking your pulse.) Try to gradually increase the intensity of your exercise. You're on safe ground as long as you are able to carry on a conversation without experiencing symptoms of overexertion (e.g., chest pain, severe shortness of breath, dizziness, nausea).

It is important for you to develop an exercise plan that you can sustain long-term. This must be taken into account when you are considering joining a gym, committing to a class, or laying out a large sum of money for equipment.

Debbie is a mother of two children under the age of 3. Last year she enrolled in an aerobics class on Wednesday evenings but found that on most Wednesday evenings either her husband worked overtime or a child was sick, limiting her attendance. She purchased exercise videos but just couldn't get motivated to use them. When discussing this problem with other young moms in the neighborhood, she discovered she wasn't alone in facing obstacles to exercise. When she suggested that the moms commit to meeting Monday, Wednesday, and Friday mornings for a half hour exercise time the other moms responded enthusiastically. The women take turns leading exercises which have varied from following a video to taking a brisk walk with the children in strollers to doing aerobics with worship music as a background. Each mom takes a turn at being the "on-call mother" to attend to any needs of the children that surface during the exercise time so that the other moms can have an uninterrupted period. The peer support has helped Debbie stick with her exercise program and has provided wonderful fellowship.

Exercise of spiritual disciplines

In addition to physical training, the exercise of the spiritual disciplines is important to enable your life to bear fruit. Just as you move your body in a conscious manner to maintain and strengthen your physical health, consciously developing your spirit will help you to maintain and strengthen the spiritual components of yourself. The spiritual disciplines include meditation, prayer, fasting, study, simplicity, solitude, submission, service, confession, worship, guidance, and celebration (Foster and Griffin, 2000). These spiritual practices are as essential to a vital state of holistic health as eating, therefore, they cannot be omitted from any discussion of a healthy lifestyle. (The spiritual disciplines will be discussed in more detail later.)

Sleep and Rest

...so on the seventh day he rested from all his work. Genesis 2:2

Come with me by yourselves to a quiet place and get some rest. Mark 6:31

Your creator appreciated the value of rest to the extent that He could put aside His work for a day. You must question what, by comparison, do *you* do that is so important that it warrants shortchanging your sleep and rest?

Periods of rest and sleep are essential to refresh and renew the body, mind, and spirit. They help you to maintain balance and a sense of well-being.

Sleep is controlled by two specialized areas of the brain:

Reticular activating system (RAS) which is associated with wakefulness

Bulbar synchronizing region (BSR) which is most active during sleep

These two systems are thought to intermittently activate and then suppress the brain centers causing periods of wakefulness and sleep.

There are two kinds of sleep: *rapid eye movement (REM)* and *non-rapid eye movement or slow wave (NREM) sleep*. A normal sleep cycle consists of four stages of NREM and a final stage of REM sleep:

Stage 1 NREM (Non-Rapid Eye Movement)

- Light sleep from which sleeper can be easily awakened
- Eyes roll from side to side
- Heart and respiratory rates slightly decrease
- Advances to next stage within several minutes if no disturbance
- Sleep interrupted during any other stage will cause cycle to return to Stage 1

Stage II NREM Sleep

- Continued light sleep with higher state of relaxation
- Sleep remains light and easily broken
- Continued decline in temperature and heart and respiratory rates
- Eyes are still

Stage III NREM Sleep

- Early stage of deep sleep
- Continued slowing of bodily processes
- Relaxation of muscles
- Moderate stimulation required to arouse sleeper

Stage IV NREM Sleep

- Extreme relaxation, deepest stage of sleep usually reached in 20-30 minutes and lasting about 30 minutes
- Decreased vital signs and body movements
- Considerable stimulation required to arouse sleeper
- This stage diminished with age and may be absent in some older adults
- It is believed that this stage is essential to physically restoring the body

REM (Rapid Eye Movement) Sleep

- Most dreaming and sleep talking occur
- Decreased tonus of head and neck muscles
- Increase and possibly irregularity of heart beat and respirations
- Electroencephalogram (EEG) resembles Stage I
- Sleepers drift into REM from Stage IV about once every 90 minutes, four to five times each night
- Can be disrupted by amphetamines, alcohol, barbiturates, or phenothiazine derivatives
- Deprivation can result in irritability, anxiety, acute psychotic episodes

Rest is a period of inactivity and peace. A period of inactivity doesn't necessarily mean you are resting. (If you've ever laid in bed in the middle of the night thinking about something you needed to do the following day you understand this!) Peace of mind promotes rest and sleep. God wants you to have peace of mind and invites you to pray and petition him for this. *Do not be anxious about anything, but in everything, by prayer and petition, with thanksgiving, present your requests to God* (Philippians 4:6). Have sufficient faith in God to turn your worries over to him.

Let's look at your typical day. Do you awaken refreshed and ready to face the day or with the feeling that you could use several more hours of sleep? If you find that you lack energy and enthusiasm, self-assess for factors that could be interfering with your sleep and rest (later in the book you'll be given a tool to help you with this assessment), such as:

- high fat, high sugar diet
- insufficient daytime activities
- too many or too lengthy daytime naps
- too much caffeine
- too much alcohol intake
- poorly managed pain
- breathing or circulatory conditions
- urinary tract disorders
- depression
- anxiety
- medications
- dissatisfaction or troubles with your job or relationships
- feeling disconnected from God, spiritually depleted

If any of these factors are in your life, consider the relationship these may have to your sleep and rest pattern.

There are some practical ways you can promote sleep and rest such as:

- establishing a regular bedtime
- meditating

- getting some exercise in the late afternoon and early evening
- limiting caffeine and alcohol intake
- spending some time outdoors during the day
- drinking an herbal tea that does not contain caffeine (e.g., chamomile, valerian)
- adjusting the environment (e.g., controlling noise, reducing lighting)
- taking a warm bath about one hour before bedtime
- receiving a massage

If you are having trouble sleeping, you need to explore the reason, so that you can do something about that.

> *Over lunch, several friends were discussing how "middle age was catching up with them" because they were turning into bed earlier and earlier each night. With that, Darlene pulled a brochure from her pocketbook. "I just heard about this co-enzyme supplement used for jet lag and chronic fatigue syndrome," Darlene shared, "and I'm thinking of using it." "You don't have chronic fatigue syndrome and you haven't been on a plane this year," her friends teasingly responded. "I know," said Darlene, "but I haven't slept well for months."*
>
> *Several months prior, Darlene's last child left for college. On closer inspection, Darlene's sleep problems could stem from her feelings about her changing family roles and reduced physical activity now that she had no children at home to pick up after and care for.*

Darlene could benefit more from seeking clarity and opportunities to use her gifts and talents instead of just treating the symptoms.

Manage Stress

You need to develop effective ways to manage the stress which confronts you in an average day. Getting proper rest and eating a nutritious diet can boost your ability to manage stress, as can doing deep breathing exercises, slowly counting to ten, diverting your attention, scheduling your time realistically, and saying a short prayer. (Some of the items listed under *Emotional and Spiritual* on the self-assessment you'll do later can be the cause and the result of stress, so see if you have any of them listed and try to examine how you can improve them.)

Solitude

Carving out time alone is a wonderful way to keep stress from overwhelming your life. Although the spiritual discipline of solitude is not intended to be a stress management technique, solitary time can help you to clear your head, gain insight into your life and your relationships, and deepen your faith walk. During periods of silence you can gain insights into behaviors that keep your life from being balanced and fruitful. You can seek solitude in several ways:

- Schedule a day of complete solitude once each month. Go away if you can; if that is not possible, stay home and ask other family members to find activities out of the house that day, unplug the phone, refrain from checking email or regular mail. (Before claiming that you just couldn't find a day each month to be alone, just consider the time you spend in unessential activities, such as window shopping and watching television, and try to shift your priorities.)
- Build at least one-half hour of personal quiet time into each day. The morning, before the rest of the family rises, can be a good time and has the added advantage of getting you centered to face the day.

- If you work or are engaged in activities outside the home, decompress and take 15 minutes alone between the time you come home and the time you start home chores.
- Designate a room or chair that the rest of your family can identify as your "quiet time place." When you occupy this space it signifies that this is your time alone and that you shouldn't be interrupted.
- Reduce routine distractions. Turn off the car radio and use driving time for reflection. Avoid having television and radios playing as background noise.

By making time and space available, you can nurture your spiritual connections and be nourished in return.

References

Foster, R. Celebration of Discipline, 2d ed, San Francisco: Harper Collins, 2009.

Study Questions

1. Pay attention to television commercials and advertisements. In what way is the message conveyed that doing is superior to being?

2. What are the major sources of stress in your life? How do you manage them? What could you do to manage them better?

3. Do you take time out during your day for solitude or "quiet time"? If not, what prevents you from doing so?

4. What type of activities could you engage in routinely to increase your opportunities for physical exercise?

CHAPTER 3

Connecting with Self and Others

Go out into the world today and love the people you meet.
Let your presence light new light in the hearts of people.
~Mother Teresa~

The supermarket checkout line offers a regular test of my ability to practice the qualities I aspire to, such as patience, turning the other cheek, and loving my neighbor. I fail the test...often! Inevitably there will be a person ahead of me in the *10 item or less* line with a load of groceries that could stock a restaurant for months. Or, there is the person who didn't buy the item for which her coupon applies and I have to wait as she "just takes a minute" to stroll to aisle 8 to exchange the item. If there are no customers holding up progress, the clerk will decide to organize the register drawers just as I approach. I bite my tongue and urge myself to set a good example; however, the message fails to be absorbed. My body language has no problem conveying the annoyance that I may not be expressing with words. Everyone in my presence gets the message. I have connected.

We connect with others in many ways, some great and some destructive. The quality of those connections rests largely on our self-awareness and self-care. In other words, we need to connect effectively with ourselves to effectively connect with others.

Connecting with Yourself

Connection with yourself is significant to your health. This entails a realistic appraisal of your sense of worth, motivators, thoughts, and feelings. Characteristics can exist that do not serve you well. This conversation between two neighbors exemplifies some of the problems that can exist.

Marg had just parked her car when she noticed Tess, her next door neighbor, pull in her driveway with a brand new Mercedes Benz. Marg walked over to congratulate Tess on her latest acquisition.

"Wow…that is a beauty!" exclaimed Marg.

"Sure is," replied Tess, "and fully loaded with every imaginable option."

"Can't hide money, can you?" teased Marg.

"Marg you earn the same as I. "How come you don't treat yourself to a new luxury car instead of buying the economy models?" asked Tess.

"Well Tess," Marg responded, "I personally don't think God wants me to use my money to buy fancy things for myself. I just don't think I deserve it. After all, my old Chevy will take me to the same places as your new Mercedes. I'd rather have a seat in heaven in the future than one in a Mercedes today."

"The way I see it," Tess quipped, "God has nothing to do with it. He didn't leave his house at the crack of dawn and put in ten hours a day at a crazy job, I did! I earned it, so who better than I should enjoy it?"

Tess' perspective that she alone is responsible for receiving and enjoying the material blessings in her life reflects an overestimation of herself. Yet, Marg's attitude leaves much to be desired as well for she is implying that she doesn't deserve to spend the money she has earned, and that God doesn't want people to enjoy nice things. Neither the extremes of an inflated ego nor a lack of self-worth is desirable. It is useful to examine yourself to identify misguided attitudes.

Purpose

The world offers you a generous smorgasbord of blueprints for living your life. Bookshelves are bulging with "how-to" books that can guide you in achieving wealth, exercising, and finding eternal youth. The lecture circuit offers a vast array of charismatic speakers who provide formulas for everything from enjoying perfect relationships to realizing your potential. Well-intentioned friends and family share their perspectives on the best choices for jobs, neighborhoods, and spouses. Schools steer students to the "right" schools for the "right" careers. You will not go wanting for advice regarding planning the direction of your life.

However, life is an adventure of an unfolding special plan for you. This plan reflects your own unique journey, ideally based on what you sense your calling and passion to be. Living your purpose aligned with a greater call may cause you to take actions that are inconsistent with the world's views of success. Consider the following example:

Fran had gone to a hospital-based nursing program fresh out of high school and graduated with flying colors. She and Bill married shortly after her graduation. By working as a RN, Fran was able to support Bill as he completed his college degree and save the down payment for their first home. Shortly after Bill took his first full-time job, Fran became pregnant with the first of their four children.

Bill's income provided the means for the couple to realize their desire to have Fran be a stay-at-home mom. Fran enjoyed this role and felt highly satisfied until the last of the kids left for college. Fran felt that she wanted to return to the profession she loved but realized that much had changed in nursing in the more than two decades since she had worked. After considerable thought and encouragement from her family, Fran enrolled in a program that enabled her to build on her experience and obtain a college degree in nursing in two years.

Fran was stimulated by her college courses and particularly liked to apply her classroom theory to her "real life." It seemed appropriate, therefore, that when she was given an assignment to plan a community health event, she would choose her church as the site. Fran organized a team of volunteers and developed a health fair that was received with overwhelming enthusiasm. Fran realized that her nursing background combined with her relationship with the church body enabled her to address health issues in a special way that was highly satisfying to her.

Through the health fair, many health-related needs of the congregation surfaced, such as health education classes, volunteer training for hospice visitation, teens' babysitter preparation classes, and caregiver support. These needs weren't lost on the church leadership who shortly thereafter approached Fran about becoming their Parish Nurse upon graduation and developing health ministry programs for the church.

Among the many types of jobs she had thought about, this was not one that had made her list, however, she was intrigued by the opportunity this type of role would afford to use her gifts and talents in a special way. Despite the fact that the church could only afford to pay her a fraction of what hospital RNs earn, Fran was challenged with the offer to develop this new role within her church.

Fran's classmates couldn't understand her consideration of this offer. "You could earn triple the salary in a hospital plus have tremendous benefits," they reminded her. Many of her friends urged her to reconsider with arguments that "your education has cost a lot so you ought to get a better return on your investment" and "think of what you could do with the extra money you could earn." Despite the arguments and after prayerful consideration, Fran accepted the position with her church.

By worldly standards, Fran may seem somewhat foolish. She is not capitalizing on her education and skills to enjoy peak earnings and the lifestyle it could provide. However, Fran has aligned her life with what she considered a greater purpose for herself and has discovered deeper and fuller rewards than she ever imagined.

Discovering your purpose begins not by charting a course, but by taking time to explore your spiritual dimension through prayer, meditation, and periods of solitude. Through this stillness an inner voice may be heard that clarifies what is truly important and feeds your spirit. The path may not be that which brings maximum income and fame, but rather, work that is compatible with one's body, mind, and spirit, and offers priceless rewards. (And, it is not uncommon for financial rewards to result from doing that you love and, consequently, do with enthusiasm and commitment.)

Work

Work plays such a major role in the lives of most people that the relationship between your work and your health warrants examination. Do you view your work as purposeful, satisfying, and energizing, or does it drain your body, mind, and spirit? One factor that could be responsible for your work being more burdensome than rewarding is that your work isn't suited for your giftedness.

Each of us has different types of *spiritual gifts* which include:

- Wisdom
- Knowledge
- Teaching
- Administration
- Leading
- Helping
- Mercy
- Faith
- Healing
- Prophecy
- Evangelism

No one gift is more important than another, and all are needed in our world. However, you can feel out of balance if you are placed in roles in which you lack opportunities to exercise your gift or where you're expected to show strength in an area in which you are not gifted.

In the five years that she worked for the insurance agency,
Emily became known for her way with people. She invested time in
learning about clients and listening to their problems. In addition, she

knew every aspect of the agency's operations, from when supplies needed to be ordered to where to find the water shut-off valve, and assumed responsibility for assuring things ran smoothly so that her boss could do his job without being bothered by trivia.

The firm's business grew significantly and the two person office grew to a staff of fifteen. The agency's owner realized that the agency needed someone to oversee the daily operations that he didn't have the time to do. Her history with the agency and people skills landed Emily the job of Office Manager.

Despite her years of outstanding work and commitment to doing a good job, Emily soon began to have difficulties in her new role. She missed the direct contact with clients and when she would hear an employee talking on the phone with a client she knew, Emily would pick up the extension and find out how the person was doing. In an effort to be helpful, Emily would perform tasks that should have been delegated to her staff. When her employees were performing at a below average level, Emily wasn't comfortable confronting them, but rather, would find excuses for their behaviors. She often would spend time trying to help staff with their personal problems and fall behind in the reports she needed to produce for the owner.

It didn't take long for things to crash. Emily's staff interpreted her lack of delegation as meaning that she didn't trust them and wasn't interested in giving them opportunities for growth. They resented her intruding on their conversations with clients. Emily was so busy doing everyone else's work that her own work was not being completed. Her reluctance to counsel and discipline poor performing employees resulted in declining productivity and lost business. The owner was frustrated that he was having to invest time dealing with dissatisfied employees and disrupted operations. Emily reached the point that she hated to come to work in the morning.

Much like Emily, having a poor fit between your giftedness and your work can lead you to be frustrated and ineffective. Granted, you may not be able to find the ideal job for your giftedness. For example, you may have the gift of teaching and find delight being in a classroom setting yet find that a teacher's salary in the local schools isn't sufficient for your needs. If you have determined that you can do nothing more to reduce expenses and you need to be employed at a job that produces higher earnings, perhaps you can seek a position in a corporation's human resources department where your gift can be used; another option is to teach a class in the community related to an area of interest or lead a Bible study at your church so that you have an outlet for expression of your gift.

Sexual Fulfillment

The norms for sexuality and sexual function have been tested and stretched to the point that our society conveys the message that sexual normality is an individual determination: there is no right or wrong, nor normal or abnormal. Interestingly, as acceptance of any type of sexual expression has increased, so have the rates of children born into single-parent homes, teen pregnancies, divorce, and sexually-transmitted diseases.

Although it may be challenged by individuals who doubt or reject the existence of God, there is biblical wisdom that not only makes sense, but that has guided healthy sexual behavior for centuries. For example, an exploration of the Bible offers insight into God's expectations regarding normal sexual function. For instance:

- *Do you not know that your body is a temple of the Holy Spirit, who is in you, whom you have received from God? You are not your own; you were bought at a price. Therefore, honor God with your body.* 1 Corinthians 6:19-20

- *It is God's will that you should be sanctified; that you should avoid sexual immorality; that each of you should learn to control his own body in a way that is holy and honorable…* 1 Thessalonians 4:3
- *You shall not commit adultery.* Exodus 20:14
- *You must not bring the earnings of a female prostitute or of a male prostitute into the house of the Lord your God to pay any vow, because the Lord your God detests them both.* Deuteronomy 23:18
- *The husband should fulfill his marital duty to his own wife, and each woman her husband.* 1 Corinthians 7:3
- *Do not deprive each other except by mutual consent and for a short time, so that you may devote yourselves to prayer. Then come together again so that Satan will not tempt you because of your lack of self-control.* 1 Corinthians 7:5
- *If a man marries his sister, the daughter of either his father or his mother, and they have sexual relations, it is a disgrace.* Leviticus 20:17
- *Flee from sexual immorality.* 1 Corinthians 6:18

God established these norms of sexual behavior because He created the sanctity of marriage and the family, and wanted to protect people from the disease, pain, and turmoil that results from sexual sins. For people of faith, honoring these norms demonstrates love and obedience to God and promotes a healthy, balanced, life.

Normally, one's ability to engage in and enjoy sexual activity is not lost with age, however, there are several changes in the female reproductive system that increase the risk for uncomfortable conditions and could interfere with satisfying sexual experiences. There is a decrease in sexual responsiveness and a reduction in the frequency of orgasm. Dyspareunia (painful intercourse) often occurs as a result of less lubrication, decreased elasticity, and thinning of the vaginal walls. (Vaginal lubricants can do much to compensate for these changes.)

Many women gain a new interest in sex after menopause, possibly because they no longer have to fear an unwanted pregnancy or because they have more time and privacy with their children grown and gone.

Sexual activity in women can be affected by their partners as the male reproductive system also experiences changes that can affect sexual function. For example, more time is required for an erection to be achieved and it is more easily lost than in younger men. Although individual differences occur in the intensity and duration of sexual response in older people, regular sexual expression for both sexes is important in promoting sexual capacity and maintaining sexual function.

Women Afire can experience a renewed or new interest and engagement in sex. Taking initiative for nurturing this aspect of self is an important action. One of the first steps may be to address the script in your head that affects your perception of yourself as a sensuous being. It is interesting how many women accept and continue to be attracted to their spouses who have grown gray, bald, and flabby, but see their own image in the mirror as being an undesirable eyesore. Accept and celebrate the body you have. Although your partner may give a long look at the stunning 25 year old, he will be aroused by and appreciate the warm, soft body that rubs against him in bed, even though she doesn't have an hour glass figure and smooth skin.

Learn about what brings you sexual pleasure so that you can share this with your partner. Asking him to softly caress your nipples or guiding his hand to your clitoris not only enables you to obtain an enjoyable sexual experience, but often excites your partner.

With good health and the availability of a partner, sexual activity can continue well into the seventh decade and beyond. But sex isn't just about intercourse. Sexuality encompasses much more than physical acts. It includes love, warmth, caring, and sharing between individuals; seeing beyond gray hair, wrinkles, and other manifestations of aging; and the intimate exchange of words and touches by sexual human beings. Feeling important to and wanted by another person promotes security, comfort, and emotional well-being. A general good health state, positive self-concept, and openness to express and receive love influence sexual function.

Solitude

"Mom, remember that you have to drive me and the guys to school today" shouted Meg's son from the hallway. Not only had she not remembered, but Meg realized that she also had a few extra phone calls to make prior to going to her office this morning. With a coffee mug, briefcase, and three teenage boys in tow, Meg raced from the house. The boys' chatter and new CD dashed any hopes of being able to make any phone calls from the car until the stop at school. Meg had barely pulled out of the school lot when her cell phone rang. She recognized her associate's number and answered to learn what the problem was. After two more phone calls and miles of rush hour traffic, Meg finally reached the office. She checked her voice mail messages while removing her coat and realized two calls needed to be made before entering her meeting. Fortunately, the 21 emails in her Inbox consisted of nothing that couldn't wait until later. As she walked to the meeting she was joined by a few coworkers who wanted to chat about the new vacation policy that had been posted. After a morning-long intense meeting, Meg decided to go out for lunch to clear her mind. She found lines at the first two restaurants she went to so she opted for a soda and hot dog from a street vendor. The only free seat Meg could find in the park was

an end of a bench which also was occupied by a couple in the midst of a heated argument. She gulped down her lunch and weaved through the crowds to return to her office for an afternoon of more of the same, all the while forming a mental list of the groceries she needed to purchase on the way home for tonight's dinner.

Your days may be similar to Meg's in that you often are engaged in some activity from the time you awaken until the time you lay your head on the pillow; even then your brain may be racing with thoughts of things you have to do, people you need to see. Voice mails, cell phones, emails, faxes, and pagers have afforded the opportunity to communicate so easily that you are bombarded with contact. You often confront crowds at the malls, office complexes, and fast food restaurants that you frequent. Within your home, simultaneously played television, music, and video games can be creating a constant din. The sensory stimulation is unrelenting. You would think that you are a human *doing* rather than a human *being*.

However, when you stop doing and allow yourself to *be* in the moment you afford yourself a rich opportunity for spiritual growth. Solitude provides the forum for this to happen. It is when you remove yourself from the *busy-ness* of daily life that you can be still and quiet enough to truly communicate with your spiritual dimension.

Connecting with Others

Once you are in a right relationship with your Higher Power and in touch with yourself, you will be in a position to enjoy a healthy connection to others.

We are created as relational beings and meant to connect with one another. *"Sure,"* you may say, *"I am around people all day. I see dozens of people at work, bump elbows with dozens more at the cafeteria, can barely find space to walk in the mall, and have other people living under the same roof with me."* Although you may come in contact with many people during the course of your day, you actually may not be connecting with them.

To a large extent, our society promotes separatism and individualism. I certainly confess to seeing many examples of this in my own life. My husband and I live on several acres in a comfortable-sized home. Most of our neighbors live in similar properties. Months can pass before neighbors have occasion to see one another. I shop at several different supermarkets (depending on where I happen to be driving at the time!) where I seldom know the clerks. Voice mails have allowed me to exchange multiple messages without actually having to speak to a living being, and the internet has enabled me to research, shop, and conduct considerable business with no human contact. I can amuse myself with video games that I can play solo and enjoy movies in the comfort and privacy of my own livingroom.

I contrast this to my parents' life. They lived in an inner city rowhouse in a Greek community where neighbors not only knew each other, but usually knew what village others came from "in the Old Country." It was not unusual to see several generations living under one roof. If a neighbor was sick, lost a job, or had a fight with a spouse, word quickly spread and you could rest assured that someone would be visiting that household to offer help or advice. I knew that I'd better be on good behavior when outside my home as the other adults in the community wouldn't hesitate to correct me as though I belonged to them. When it rained and someone had clothes hanging on the line, the nearest neighbor would take them down if the lady of the house was out; the neighbor also would enter the house and close any opened windows because of course, no one locked their doors. My mother shopped at the local grocery store that had been operated by the same family for decades. If my friends and I were short of change to pay for our purchases at the local drug store, the pharmacist, who knew us since we were carried in our mothers' arms, would tell us just to make it good the next time we came in. There were many "characters" whose peculiarities and flaws seasoned the atmosphere, but who were tolerated---and cared about by their neighbors. When the weather allowed, the most popular form of recreation was sitting in the back yard or on the front steps where the neighborhood adults would share news and life stories, and the kids would play catch, jacks, and dodge ball. Although I'm not claiming that this life was free of problems, there was a richness to living in community. Although it can be more challenging for us than previous generations, living a life that promotes holistic health demands that we experience the richness of healthy connections.

It is useful to take time to reflect on the relationships that have formed the weaving the tapestry of your life. Through relationships, we show our Creator's love and see His love manifested in a variety of ways. Various studies have demonstrated higher levels of health and improvements in health conditions when individuals are engaged in loving, supportive relationships (e.g., married people have lower suicide rates that those who are alone; married men live longer than single men). Good relationships can teach, encourage, inspire, expand, and restore us.

Examine your relationships. Healthy relationships reflect mutual trust, respect, caring, honesty, and sharing. They are nonjudgmental and provide a safe haven for growth. In contrast, unhealthy relationships can be characterized by distorted boundaries between the individuals, one person sacrificing self to please the other person, a lack of forgiveness, one family member stifling the growth and independence of another, or physical, emotional, sexual, or financial abuse.

Showing love, forgiveness, acceptance, and tolerance in your relationships is important, yet that does not mean you must allow yourself to be subjected to the abusive, destructive, or sinful behaviors of others. When you are faced with these situations some useful measures could include:

- *Examining your role.* Consider what you may be communicating through your words and actions---and through what you do not say and do---that could be giving the other person an incorrect message. For example, if you have a friend who repeatedly tells her spouse that she is spending time with you when she actually is spending that time engaging in an adulterous relationship, and expects that you'll cover for her, examine what message you have conveyed that could have been interpreted as your acceptance of this arrangement. You may not like to be placed in this situation but perhaps are uncomfortable confronting your friend and instead beat around the bush by saying, "Well, you know this isn't right, but okay, just this time"; or maybe you've inadvertently encouraged the relationship by making comments such as "He does seem to treat you better than your husband."

- *Seeking counsel.* Discuss the matter with a trusted friend, counselor, or your clergy who can offer insights.

- *Confronting the matter.* Ignoring unhealthy actions that impact you serves no good purpose. Discuss the issue with the individual, kindly and gently. Rather than attack the person with judgmental statements (e.g., "You'll go to hell for your actions." "You're a horrible person." "Your kids will hate you for what you're doing."), present the issue from the perspective of how you feel (e.g., "It hurts me when you treat me this way," "I feel uncomfortable being asked to lie for you as I believe it is the wrong thing to do," "I care for you as a friend and it grieves me to see you committing adultery.") Be direct.

- *Offering paths to changing the situation.* Provide suggestions for resources (e.g., counseling, support groups, AA, etc.) that can assist. Offer to pray for and with the person, if appropriate. Ask the person for insights and suggestions that can aid in the resolution.

- *Praying.* Ask God to reveal the truth and guide you in doing what is right. He often can show paths to correcting a bad situation that you couldn't have considered on your own. Assuring that you provide adequate time to *listen* to God speak to you during prayer time is crucial.

There may be a situation in which there is a person in your life who:

- repeatedly asks and receives favors from you but doesn't reciprocate
- is cruel and critical of you and/or loved ones
- belittles you in front of others
- absorbs considerable amounts of your time discussing her life but has no interest in hearing about yours
- makes regular requests for you to do things on her behalf that violate your values

Such relationships are toxic and eat away at you emotionally and spiritually. If confronting the matter and requesting a change in behavior does not bring about improvements, it may be time to do some emotional Spring Cleaning and rid yourself of their relationships. It is important to disengage yourself from relationships that depress, degrade, or demoralize you.

Connection with others offers concrete health benefits, also. The past two decades have shown a growth in our understanding of *psychoneuroimmunology*---a branch of science that describes the relationship of one's psychological state to the immune system. Studies have found that:

- Social support reduces the negative psychological and physiological effects of stress (Uchino et al, 1996)
- Emotional support from family and friends buffers stressful life events, reduces the risk of depression, and hastens recovery from depression (George 1992)
- People recovering from heart attacks who had emotional support were less likely to die than persons without any source of support (Berkman, 1995)
- Women with metastatic breast cancer who participated in a support group where they could share experiences, feelings, and advice lived twice as long as comparable women who did not attend support groups (Spiegel, 1989)
- Social isolation of primates adversely affects the immune system function and increases susceptibility to disease (Sapolsky et al, 1997)

Extensive research supports that living in a right relationship to self and others has multiple benefits.

It can be helpful to create an image in your mind of echoes and mirrors when you think about your relationships in that what you get back depends on what you give.

Suggestions for Healthy Relationships

- Recognize that you influence others whether you realize it or not.
- Tame your tongue and think before you speak.
- Choose to love rather than be driven by emotional needs.
- Offer time for responses and reactions to surface.

- Put others first.
- Be humble.
- Avoid judgmental behavior and revenge; repay evil with love and good deeds.
- Honor commitments.
- Be hospitable and find ways to serve others.
- Foster peace and harmony.
- Appreciate diversity in attributes, giftedness, behaviors.
- Communicate assertively.
- Resolve conflict in a win-win manner.
- Speak about your feelings rather than expressing judgments.
- Present complaints in the form of suggestions or requests.
- Show grace and give the benefit of the doubt.
- Take time to reflect and understand.
- Forgive and move on.
- Know when to prune relationships.
- Encourage, empower, and build up others.
- Respect others, remembering each are God's children.

Connecting with Nature

The first chapter of Genesis describes how God took nothingness and created light, sky, sun, moon, stars, water, plants, trees, fish, birds, and a wide array of living creatures. God took pride in His creation, judging it to be good. He then gave the apex of His creation, man and woman, the gift of this vast, wondrous creation---to inhabit, tend, and enjoy.

It is useful for your physical, mental, and spiritual well-being to spend time enjoying nature each day. This could be accomplished through a walk in the park, driving home from work on a scenic route (even if it takes a little longer!), gardening, or sitting outside on your porch. Take a few minutes to allow your senses to experience the wonderful surroundings: listen to birds chirping, take in a deep breath and notice the scent of the grass and flowers, stroke the petal of a flower.

Connection with nature fosters your connection to God, also. It is difficult to see the spectacular colors of a sunset, gaze across a body of water that seems to go on forever, hear birds chirping their unique songs, or smell the fragrance of blossoming flowers without feeling awestruck at the superb craftsmanship of God. You honor Him by enjoying the products of His creation.

Connecting through Prayer

If you are a woman of faith you appreciate the significance of prayer and should incorporate it into your day as much as possible. On your way to a meeting or to work, ask God for guidance, patience, and understanding. As you're sitting in rush hour traffic going nowhere fast, use the time to offer prayers of praise. Communicate with God as you take a walk. Affirm your love for God throughout the day. Confess your wrongdoings and keep a short account with God.

It is helpful to schedule time for prayer or meditation in the same manner as any other important or essential activity in your life. The time you spend in prayer or meditation can help you to get focused and centered, and approach the day with a positive attitude, knowing you will not have to face your challenges alone.

A wonderful routine to establish is to engage in some quiet time for prayer or meditation before launching into your daily routines. I find that as an early-riser, my best time is in the morning hours before my husband stirs, the phone begins ringing, and the responsibilities of the day absorb my attention. I use this time to read devotionals and pray. Spending this quiet time with the Lord starts my day on a grounded, peaceful footing and enables me to be more aware of His presence with me throughout the day than if I rushed into my daily activities without prayer. I compare it to having a guest in my home who will be accompanying me throughout the day. With this special person by my side, I tend to be more thoughtful of my words and actions than when I'm alone. Likewise, a conscious effort to connect with the Lord in the morning and invite Him to accompany me through the day cause me to be aware of the way in which my words and actions affect Him.

There is no right or wrong way to pray. God is more interested in your honest, open relationship with Him than He is in you following a specific protocol for praying. There are as many various styles of prayer as there are people who pray. Prayer can include talking (aloud or silently), meditating on scripture verses, listening for God to speak, crying, chanting, singing, or being acutely aware of the present moment. Its components can include:

- acknowledgement of the wonders of God's power, grace, and mercy;
- expressions of adoration and appreciation for all God has offered;
- petitions to God for specific needs and guidance;
- confession of sins; and
- requests on behalf of others.

Regardless of the style or content of your prayers, make them a frequent and active part of your daily routines.

Laugh!

A cheerful heart is good medicine, but a crushed spirit dries up the bones. Proverbs 17:22

Humor and optimism have a positive impact on your health state. The act of laughing produces physiological effects that can be beneficial; these effects include:

- Increased heart rate and circulation
- Increased respirations and oxygenation of tissues
- Exercise of thoracic and abdominal muscles
- Release of endorphins which is helpful in improving mood, reducing pain sensations, decreasing anxiety, and relieving muscle tension
- Increased metabolism
- Stimulation of the immune system

Find ways for laughter to permeate your life and the lives you touch. Share jokes and funny stories. If you're not skilled at remembering or delivering jokes, try keeping a scrapbook of clippings of funny stories and jokes that you can tap when needed. Include an abundance of comedies among your movie selections. Rent videos of old *I Love Lucy, Candid Camera, Marx Brothers, Laurel and Hardy,* and other classics. Read humorous books. Spend time with children. Be playful and smile often.

Very importantly, don't take yourself too seriously. Be willing to laugh at yourself, particularly when you make stupid mistakes. You have a choice as to the manner in which you react to the unpleasant incidents in your life. You can become angry and complain, or find the humor in the situation and take it lightly. Finding the humor in the situation gives you a sense of control. Further, it influences the mood of those around you and can aid in reducing the stress of yourself and others.

References

Berkman L. The role of social relations in health promotion. Psychosomatic Medicine 57:245-   254, 1995.

Foster RJ and Griffin E. Spiritual Classics.   Selected Readings for Individuals and Groups on the Twelve Spiritual Disciplines. New York: HarperSanFrancisco, 2000.

George LK. Social factors and the onset and outcome of depression. In KW Schaie, D Blazer,   and JS House (eds), Aging, Health Behaviors, and Health Outcomes, pp 137-159).   Hillsdale, NJ: Lawrence Erlbaum Associates, 1992.

Sapolsky RM, Alberts SC, and Altman J. Hypercortisolism associated with social subordinance   or social isolation among wild baboons. Archives of General Psychiatry, 54: 1137-1143,   1997.

Spiegel D. et al. Effect of psychosocial treatment on survival of patients with metastatic breast cancer. Lancer 2: 888_891, 1989.

Uchino BN, Cacioppo JR, and Kiecolt-Glaser JK. The relationship between social support and   physiological processes. A review with emphasis on underlying mechanisms and implications   for health. Psychological bulletin, 119: 488-531, 1996.

Study Questions

1. What examples have you experienced yourself or seen in others in which emotional or spiritual distress affected physical health?

2. Examine a group in which you are a member (e.g., family, work group, committee). How are the various spiritual gifts represented? What are the risks of not having a good representation of the various spiritual gifts?

3. What are some of the consequences you witness in society of people violating biblical principles of sexuality?

4. What are the differences between loneliness and being alone?

5. What are some ways that you can celebrate nature?

6. How much time do you devote to solitude? If it is insufficient, what measures can you take to increase it.

CHAPTER 4

Committing to Being Healthy

The idea is to die young as late as possible.
~Ashley Montagu~

*D*o you want to get well? When Jesus posed this question to the invalid man by the pool (John 5:6) He implied that the man had a choice to change his condition. Likewise, we have some control over the state of our health. But, like the invalid man, we must do more than possess an understanding of what good health means; we must make conscious decisions and take specific actions to reflect that we want to be well.

Believing You Can Be Healthy

What does it mean to you to believe in something? Usually you have faith or confidence in something in which you believe. You trust that it can be depended upon to be true and often proceed with actions confidently based on that understanding. For example, you believed that the chair you are sitting on could hold your weight and seated yourself without hesitancy. You acted based on your beliefs.

Your values provide a frame of reference for your beliefs. Values consist of your standards and that which has worth to you. They offer meaning and direction. The Bible provides the foundation for the values that people of faith hold.

The state of your health can be influenced significantly by the beliefs you hold and, in turn, your health-related beliefs can be influenced significantly by the worldview of the society in which you live. You may have given the relationship between the worldview and your beliefs little thought, but the prevailing worldview has impacted you. When it comes to matters of health, our society has valued the scientific approach---the *biomedical model*---characterized by the following:

- *Mechanism:* the human body is explained in terms of physics and chemistry and considered to operate much like a machine. Health is determined by physical structure and function, and disease is a malfunction of the physical part. Malfunctions and malformations are undesirable. Disease is treated by repairing the malformed or malfunctioning organ or system with physical or chemical interventions (e.g., drugs, surgery). God has no role in one's health state or healing, and dysfunction and deformity have no purpose.
- *Materialism:* the human body and its state of health are influenced only by what can be seen and measured. Illness is caused by a physical malfunction and is addressed by concrete treatments. One's emotional and spiritual states have no impact on health and healing.

- *Reductionism*: the human body is viewed in terms of isolated parts. Treatment of a health condition addresses the individual organ or system rather than the whole being. One can have good health by having body systems that functioned well, despite spiritual state.

Within these belief systems, you could be considered healthy in the absence of a relationship with God or a Higher Power. Further, illness, deformity, and disability serve no purpose.

In recent years the biomedical model has been challenged by a *holistic model* which is based on the beliefs that:

- Each person is a highly individualized being made of body, mind, and spirit.
- A person's body, mind, and spirit are interrelated.
- Health is judged by wholeness and harmony of the body, mind, and spirit and not merely the absence of disease.
- The treatment of disease addresses and utilizes the resources of the body, mind, and spirit.
- Disease can serve a purpose.

If you're like many people, at some time in your life you've made impressive plans for self-improvement on New Year's Eve, only to have them abandoned by mid-February. Many intentions to improve health are doomed from the start because of the lack of belief in the ability to change or succeed. This lack of belief is couched in comments like *"I can't find time in my schedule to shop for groceries, much less build in an exercise program or relaxation exercises,"* or, *"My mother was overweight and her mother before her, so I guess I just inherited their genes."* Excuses, blame, and rationalizations often prevent us from taking positive actions and altering the landscape of our health. Sometimes we stay in unhealthy patterns because we believe these patterns offer more comfort and security than the alternatives.

Self-Evaluation

Prior to launching your effort to improve your health, it is helpful to examine the beliefs that influence your health behaviors. The following questions will guide you in this self-evaluation.

1. What does *good health* mean to you?

2. To what degree do you see your health state as a matter of fate?

3. To what degree are you willing to change each of the following to improve your health:

   • Eating habits?

   • Amount of activity and exercise?

   • Leisure activities?

   • Quality of relationships?

   • Lifestyle?

   • Allocation of time for prayer, meditation, and solitude?

4. Deep down, do you think that you won't be affected by eating poorly, failing to exercise, shortchanging your sleep requirements, and skipping personal quiet time?

5. In regard to diet, activities, and relationships, did your family promote behaviors that ran contrary to good health practices (e.g., eating high-fat foods, tolerating abusive relationships, ignoring drunkenness of a family member)?

6. Do the benefits of looking and feeling better outweigh the sacrifices you may need to make in forfeiting unhealthy practices?

7. Do you think it is selfish to spend time relaxing and exercising, or to refuse to engage in social functions with friends and family who are draining?

8. Do you believe you can influence your current state of health?

Meaning of Health

For years, health was assumed to mean the absence of disease, but that definition has fallen by the wayside. You may realize from experiences in your own life that you can be free from any formal diagnosis of a health condition, yet not be feeling or functioning at your best. Now, as mentioned, health is viewed in terms of harmony and vitality of the body, mind, and spirit. This broader description implies that when you are healthy you:

- awaken each day with enthusiasm, energy, a sense of purpose, and a will to live
- connect with people and nature
- love and allow yourself to be loved
- accept and offer forgiveness
- have a sense of spiritual peace.

65

With this perspective, you can be healthy despite having a disease or disability. This was displayed to me many years ago when I was a teenage "Candy-Striper" in the long-term care section of what was then Baltimore City Hospital. This was the city's "charity hospital" that cared for people too poor to seek care elsewhere during the pre-Medicaid days. On one of the dingy, large wards lived a man named Charlie Toye. Mr. Toye had resided on the ward for many years before I met him and had no family. Further, he was quadriplegic and totally dependent on others for the most basic of needs. I had never seen a person like this before, and my teenage mind pondered how anyone could bear this condition. But as the weeks passed, I noticed that Mr. Toye's room seemed to be a magnet for staff. Housekeepers, nursing assistants, nurses, and maintenance workers would approach his bedside looking tired and beaten, but depart with new energy and smiles. Although he couldn't lift a finger, Mr. Toye could touch others through his attentive listening, kind words, and warm heart. This motionless man who couldn't raise food to his own mouth fed the souls of those he encountered. And he must have gotten back what he gave as he was consistently cheerful, optimistic, and positive. Years later, after completing nursing school, I returned to this hospital to work and found Mr. Toye still holding court with employees, still lifting spirits, still displaying joy. I believe Mr. Toye truly enjoyed a high level of holistic health.

Responsibility for Health

Viewing health as a matter of fate causes you to feel powerless in your ability to change the course of your life. *"It's out of my hands," "I never have any luck,"* and *"You can't change the cards you've been dealt"* are comments reflecting a fatalistic view of health. Granted, there are some realities that you cannot change, such as being born with a developmental disability.

But, you can exercise tremendous power to maximize your potential by taking care of your body, mind, and spirit. Placing responsibility for your health on fate makes no more sense than trusting the oil change in your car to fate, rather than conscious effort.

You may understand what good health practices are and have a desire to improve your health, but be unwilling to make sacrifices. *"I'll gain weight if I stop smoking." "If I no longer stop for a drink after work I'll lose contact with my friends." "I've got several small kids; I don't have time to indulge in an aerobics class."* Although you have the potential to change and adopt healthy practices, you must have the desire to do so.

Consistently following good health practices is tough; even if you're the most dedicated health advocate you most likely have occasional slips. However, you're kidding yourself if you think you can regularly make poor choices concerning your health and escape the consequences. I often encounter people who tell me: *"My parents and grandparents ate high-fat diets and they all lived to their eighties." "I've smoked cigarettes for years and get fewer colds than people who have never smoked." "I don't think these doctors know what they're talking about."* There are the rare exceptions of individuals who have abused their bodies and lived long, seemingly unimpaired lives, but for most people, poor health practices take their toll. You are a human being, not a superhuman being.

Influences on Health

Family and cultural influences are a deep part of your makeup, sprinkling your life with richness, uniqueness, and diversity. However, not all of these influences are positive in regard to your health. Maria's story is one example:

Maria was raised in an Italian home in which food played an important part. Her mother spent hours preparing dinners, and her father released stress from his hectic job in the factory by feasting on the elaborate meals. Having lived through the Great Depression, Maria's parents viewed a plump frame as a sign of health and well-being, and encouraged their children to eat heartedly. By the time she was in her teens, Maria was significantly obese.

When she went away to college, Maria learned about the principles of good nutrition and successfully shed her excess weight. On her first visit home, her parents were critical of her slim appearance and tempted her with her past favorite foods. When she refused the fattening treats, her mother pouted and her father accused her of "thinking she was too good for the family now that she was a college girl."

In a family like Maria's, people may develop unhealthy eating habits because compliance with family norms yields love and acceptance. Likewise, if as a child you observed most men stopping in the corner tavern for a few drinks each day after work and their wives merely shaking their heads when their spouses staggered home, you could become an adult who abuses or tolerates the abuse of alcohol in your own home. Unhealthy chains must be broken.

You may find yourself running in a maze of unhealthy practices. You know you should eat fresh wholesome foods yet grabbing pizza or burgers at the local carryout is much easier. You realize your waistline is spreading and that you're getting winded climbing stairs, yet you opt to spend your free time in front of the television rather than walking or engaging in some other form of exercise. You see that family time has shrunk to dangerously low levels to accommodate the demands of your job, but feel you need to invest the extra time and energies in work to be competitive. You recognize that time spent with certain relatives who are negative and critical is unpleasant and stressful yet you feel you "should" have regular contact with them. You may continue unhealthy habits because these are quicker, easier, or more comfortable than doing what you know to be right. Unfortunately, these habits contribute to a compromised state of health that potentially can:

- lead to a less than fully productive life
- impose burdens on others
- destroy your family
- divert your attention from worthwhile pursuits to fruitless and even harmful activities

You may view time spent in resting, exercising, and solitude as selfish activities. After all, how can you indulge in spending an afternoon in solitude when you could be taking the grandkids to the zoo? Or, what kind of person would you be if you set limits and refused to listen to a friend who chronically complains about a problem while doing nothing to correct the situation? Taking care of yourself is responsible, not selfish. If you are to follow God's command to *love others as yourself* you must assure you are demonstrating healthy self-love through responsible actions with your body, mind, and spirit so that you are equipped to love and serve well.

Safety

Air pollution…crime…terrorists…tainted meats…tornadoes…. The world is full of hazards, many of which are beyond your control. However, there are threats to your health and well-being that you can protect yourself against.

Your first line of defense is to keep yourself healthy. Many of the measures already discussed, such as good nutrition, adequate rest, and regular exercise contribute to your health and can assist in giving you resistance against illness.

Boosting your immunity is an important measure and far surpasses treating infections and diseases after they have invaded your body. As you get older and when you have a chronic health problem, such as emphysema or diabetes, you have a higher than normal risk for developing infections. You need to actively prevent them by strengthening your immunity. Some ways in which you can enhance the function of your immune system are offered below. In addition, be careful not to overuse antibiotics. Overuse of antibiotics can disrupt the body's natural balance and enable new infections to develop (as women who have developed vaginal infections after using antibiotics can attest). Excess antibiotic use can cause bacteria to become resistant to these drugs, also.

STRENGTHENING THE IMMUNE SYSTEM

Diet: milk, yogurt, nonfat cottage cheese, eggs, fresh fruits and vegetables, grains, nuts, onion, sprouts, pure honey, unsulfured molasses

Herbs: echinacea, goldenseal, ginseng, garlic

Exercise: any form of moderate regular exercise

Stress management: meditation, progressive relaxation, periods of solitude

Attitude: open, assertive, trusting, altruistic, loving, appreciative

---

Safe use of complementary and alternative therapies

There has been an explosion in the use of herbal remedies, homeopathy, acupuncture, chiropractic, magnet therapy, and other complementary and alternative therapies. Complementary and alternative therapies are those health promotion and healing practices that fall outside the realm of conventional medical practice in our country. Nearly half of all Americans use some form of complementary and alternative medicine, for which they spend billions of dollars annually. You may be among the users of these therapies, but even if you're not, you probably are being bombarded with them. Alternative health gurus like Andrew Weil and Deepak Chopra are prominent in the media and just about every pharmacy and supermarket carries a line of supplements and alternative health products. The National Institutes of Health has created a National Center for Complementary and Alternative Medicine to support research and integration of these therapies into the conventional health care system.

There are legitimate reasons for the skyrocketing interest in complementary and alternative therapies. Experiences with mainstream medical care have left much to be desired by consumers as five minute impersonal office visits have replaced the warm relationship once shared with the old family doctor. Alternative therapists who invest time to learn about and listen to their clients offer a positive substitute to consumers. Many people want to use natural approaches to treat illnesses and avoid using medications and other interventions that carry high risks for complications. Americans have become aware of interesting and new healing techniques as communication and knowledge of other cultural practices have increased. Physicians, nurses, and other conventional health care professionals are integrating complementary and alternative therapies into their practices and teaching these therapies in their schools.

The popularity of complementary and alternative therapies assures that many women will encounter them and consider their use. This is especially true for women who seek alternatives to prescription hormonal replacement therapy. Discernment is essential as choices are made. Just because a therapy has been used for centuries or is promoted by a charismatic leader doesn't make it effective. Some therapies are based on the beliefs or testimonies of a small minority of people; research may be nonexistent or limited to sample sizes too small for results to be significant. The fact that a substance is "natural" doesn't mean it cannot cause harmful effects. An example is gingko biloba that people use for memory enhancement; this herb that can thin the blood and cause serious bleeding problems in some individuals. Some alternative therapists may be skilled in practicing their specific modality but lack comprehensive education that could enable them to properly recognize a wide range of health conditions; conditions may go undiagnosed and treatment delayed as a result.

Some Christians are concerned about using alternative therapies as some are based on Eastern, New Age, or other faiths that are in conflict with Christianity. These practices go against Biblical teachings and rely on sources of spiritual intervention other than Jesus Christ. Table 2 in the Appendix describes some popular complementary and alternative therapies and how they could pose problems for Christians. Below are some tips for discerning these therapies.

Checklist for Discerning Complementary and Alternative Modalities (CAM)

_____ You have obtained a conventional physical exam to understand your health state prior to using CAM.

_____ Scientific evidence exists supporting the claims made for the selected CAM.

____ The CAM practitioner works in concert with conventional medical practitioners and refers to them when needed.

____ The CAM practitioner doesn't claim that he or she possesses special healing powers and doesn't call on special spirits for healing.

____ The CAM does not require that religious systems incompatible with your own be supported or practiced.

____ The CAM practitioner is licensed or certified as required by the state.

____ The CAM product is labeled and standardized.

____ Claims of the CAM practitioner can be validated by another source.

____ The CAM practitioner allows you to purchase prescribed products from any source and does not require you purchase only from him/her

Normality

An important aspect of health involves keeping your body makeup and function within normal limits. This includes such things as assuring you have a blood pressure below 140/90, a regular heart beat, unobstructed blood circulation, and blood chemistry within a normal range. Good health practices and prompt attention to symptoms of health problems assist in maintaining normality.

In order to maintain normality, you need to be able to identify abnormalities. Sometimes, signs and symptoms alert you to the fact that something is wrong, as what occurs when you experience a fever, find a lump in your breast, or notice a significant change in your mood. However, there are many abnormalities that you cannot detect in an early stage that require special types of examinations and tests in order to be detected. Regular, comprehensive physical check-ups can aid in detecting health conditions early; some of the specific tests and exams that are important to include are:

- Blood pressure reading
- Electrocardiograph
- Laboratory analysis of blood, urine, and stool
- Rectal examination, colonoscopy
- Gynecological (GYN) exam
- Annual mammogram
- Hormonal analysis (estradiol, FSH, LH, testosterone, free testosterone) if perimenopausal or menopausal but attempting to determine replacement needs

If libido is low or sexual dysfunction is a problem blood testing of thyroid function (T3, T4, free T4, TSH), platelet MAO, and prolactin can be useful. (Discuss these with your health care provider.) In addition, you can aid in detecting health problems early by performing self-examinations of your breast. Your health care provider can explain the procedures for these self-examinations to you and you also can obtain information from your local chapter of the American Cancer Society. Be sure to have any abnormality that you note evaluated as early as possible.

Assess Where You Are

So, you say that you believe you can live a healthy abundant life? In that case, your next step is to take stock of the current state of your body, mind, and spirit. In the Appendix of this book you'll find a self assessment tool (Exhibit 1) that reviews major aspects of your health status. To do it justice, block out some uninterrupted time so that you can give some careful thought to your responses. Upon completion of this self-assessment, you'll be ready to develop a personal action plan (Exhibit 2, also in the Appendix) to improve your health.

Changing health habits is a slow and continuous process, but one with profound and long-term benefits. Keep in mind that you are seeking balance, not perfection. The exercise on the pages that follow can aid you in determining the degree of balance in your life. Begin by plotting where you'd assess yourself to be along the continuum of the 20 items listed.

Faith

10	5	1
Believe in God or Higher Power; strong relationship	Belief in God or Higher Power but occasionally doubt or feel unsure	No belief in God or Higher Power

Diet

10	5	1
Consistently eat according to recommendations daily	<2 Fruits & vegetables daily; eat "junk food" >3 times a week	Rarely eat fruits & vegetables; eat "junk food"

Fluids

10	5	1
Drink 6-8 glasses of water per day; rarely drink soda	Drink 6-8 glasses of water daily; <4 coffees or sodas daily	Drink <3 glasses of water daily; high intake coffee and/or soda

Elimination

10	5	1
Daily bowel movement without difficulty	Every other day bowel movement without difficulty	Irregularity; dependent on laxatives/ enemas

Exercise

10	5	1
15 minutes daily or at least 30 minutes 3 times/week	Less than 2 times per week	No regular exercise

Sleep/Rest

10	5	1
No problem falling or staying asleep; naps <15 minutes	Difficulty falling or staying asleep <3 times/week; irregular naps	Nightly difficulty falling or staying asleep; no naps or frequent naps lasting >30 minutes

Sex

10	5	1
Level & frequency of intimacy satisfying to self and spouse	Self or spouse dissatisfied with level or frequency	Self or spouse totally disinterested; no intimacy; adulterous; promiscuous

Prayer/Meditation

10	5	1
Daily prayer, meditation, or quiet time	Irregular prayer, meditation, or quiet time (<2 times/month)	No prayer, meditation, or quiet time

Solitude

10	5	1
At least 15 minutes of personal time daily; quarterly retreat	At least 15 minutes personal time <3 times/week; yearly retreat	No personal private time

Work/Vocation

10	5	1
Fully satisfied; using gifts and talents regularly	Occasionally dissatisfied; seldom use gifts and talents	Completely dissatisfied; rarely use gifts and talents

Purpose

10	5	1
Consistently feel life has meaning and that I have a purpose for living	Regularly question meaning of life and my purpose	Feel hopeless and that I make little difference

Leisure

10	5	1
Engage in play or hobby daily	Engage in play or hobby weekly	No hobby, seldom play

Relationships

10	5	1
Satisfying, nurturing, good balance of give and take	Often stressful but more positive than negative	Draining; stressful; negative; abusive

Connection with Nature

10	5	1
Enjoy nature (trees, birds, etc) >1 hour/week	Enjoy nature <30 minutes weekly	Enjoy nature <1 hour per month

Service

10	5	1
Consistently have helpful attitude; weekly volunteer activity	Selective helping; occasionally volunteer	Not serving; helping does not come easily

77

Study

10	5	1
Read/study activity daily for personal growth	Read/study activity weekly for personal growth	Rarely read/study for personal growth

Fasting

10	5	1
Fast from food or activity at least once/month	Fast from food or activity <3 times/year	No fasting

Celebration

10	5	1
Joyful life majority of time; regular fellowship and fun	More joyfulness than not; fellowship and fun on major holidays/celebrations	Joyless life; lack fellowship and fun

Symptoms

10	5	1
Symptom-free	Headaches, pain, indigestion, other symptoms once weekly	Daily symptoms

Health Screening

10	5	1
Prompt attention to symptoms; physical/dental/eye exams within past year; annual mammogram, monthly self-exam of breasts	Delay having symptoms evaluated; exams 1-3 years; self-exams every 2-3 months	Ignore symptoms; >3 years since last exams; no self-exams

Now, plot the score for each item on this Balance Wheel:

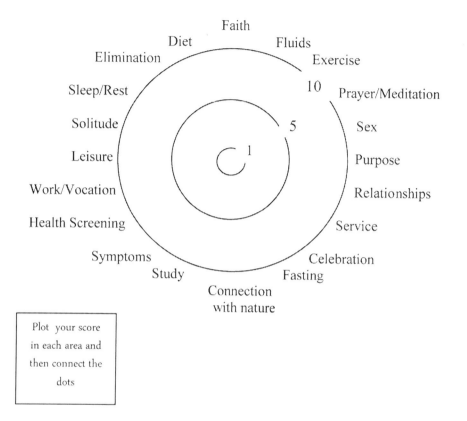

Plot your score
in each area and
then connect the
dots

You may find that your Balance Wheel lacks a completely smooth surface. Some of these imbalances may merely create minor bumps in your journey that are hardly noticeable, although in time, they can risk throwing your total being out of alignment. Others may be sufficiently deep that they are obviously disrupting your health and well-being now. Your challenge is to take responsibility for restoring and maintaining balance so that you can enjoy optimal holistic health. This begins by taking stock of where your major imbalances exist. Look over your Balance Wheel and list areas of imbalance:

Now, prioritize them. In your prioritization, consider imbalances that are causing the most interference with your ability to achieve optimal holistic health. Write the three areas that lead your list of imbalances:

1.

2.

3.

Look at them and think about them. Spend some time praying or meditating to consider the causes and impact of the imbalances.

Develop a plan for improving these three imbalances. Consider the goals or outcomes you want to achieve, actions that can assist you in getting there, and reasonable dates for achieving them. You can review chapters in this book that discuss specific areas to obtain some suggestions. Write your plan in a format similar to this:

Imbalance	Goal	Actions	Target Date

Develop a list of affirmations related to your goals. For example, if one of your goals is to spend 30 minutes walking in the park twice each week, state this in the form of an affirmative statement that puts you in the place of actually achieving it: *I spend 30 minutes walking in the park two times each week.* This sets a standard for you to achieve and conveys to your brain a message that you are actively engaging in the act. Write down these affirmations and place a copy where you will regularly see it, so that they will be active in your thoughts.

Your intention and actions to address your imbalances should help you to improve these areas of your life. You can then revisit your Balance Wheel and address other priorities.

You Do As You Believe

Your health status is influenced greatly by your beliefs. For people of faith, the first and foremost belief is that *God wants you to live an abundant life.* An abundant life doesn't guarantee a disease-free, painless existence; despite the most ideal practices, suffering and hardship can occur. Nor does it mean overflowing wealth so that you can buy expensive toys and enjoy a life of leisure. Rather, an abundant life is one in which you experience the fullness of a relationship with God and are secure in the knowledge that you will be provided with what you need and the strength to flourish through suffering and hardship.

Another belief that influences your health is that *you have the ability to change unhealthy practices and develop healthy ones.* You can break the chain of unhealthy habits that you've acquired and establish a healthy lifestyle that can serve as a positive model to your friends and family. It is never too late. Some steps that can help you in changing beliefs are to:

81

- *Journal.* Keep a written record of your struggles and accomplishments. Read through your entries and try to detect patterns, such as going off your diet whenever your mother-in-law visits or drinking a few beers when you've had a tough day at work. Recognize accomplishments, offer praise, and reward yourself.

- *Use affirmations.* Develop a few statements that positively reflect your goal. (*"I can lose 20 pounds." "I am able to relieve my stress by taking a walk rather than having a drink." "I can complete 15 minutes of exercises every morning." "I have the strength to face this challenge."*) Replace any fear of failure with a mental script for success.

- *Pray.* If you are a person of faith, build prayer into your daily routine. Ask guidance to reveal those aspects of your life that are harmful and assistance in making necessary changes. Pray for specific areas of change. (*"Lord, help me to organize my time so that I can do my exercises each day." "Father, please give me strength to resist temptation and not eat harmful foods." "Dear God, please keep my mind from wandering during my prayer time."*) Confess your shortcomings and offer praise for accomplishments. Pray with the expectation that your prayers will be answered and persist, even when you cannot see immediate results. And ask other people of faith to pray for you, as well.

The belief that you can have a healthy, abundant life serves as a foundation for all your actions and enables you to plant the seeds of success.

> *"Don't be afraid; just believe."*
>   Mark 5:36

Be Proactive

Good health practices also include smart management of your symptoms and illnesses. Think about some of the symptoms you experience (the self-assessment tool that you complete later will help you with this.) How many of them can you prevent or improve by lifestyle changes, such as changing your diet, increasing your exercise, reducing your intake of alcohol, or managing your stress more effectively? You need to consider some of the reasons that you may not have taken these actions in the past (e.g., lack of knowledge regarding good nutritional practices, poor motivation, family pressures, cultural factors) and try to work on them as you can.

We have become a society that looks for quick and easy relief in a pill. Not all medications are bad; in fact, many drugs have not only enabled people to add years to their lives, but also more life to their years. Yet, there are risks with drugs, serious risks. The side effects of a drug can cause more discomfort than the symptoms for which it was originally prescribed. And, medications can be fatal. The American Medical Association reported that drug-related reactions were the fourth leading cause of death in the United States. These comments are not meant to suggest that you not use medications, but that you use them only when necessary and appropriately. Medications should not be used as a substitute for you taking an active role in your own healing. Reducing junk foods could eliminate your need for antacids; exercising and reducing weight could cause your joints to be less painful and reduce the need for a pain reliever; spending quiet time with the Lord can relieve anxieties and eliminate the need for tranquilizers and sedatives. Some ways that you can enhance your safety in using drugs are described in Table 3 in the Appendix.

Changing your health habits isn't easy...change seldom is! However, we have a duty to care for the bodies, minds, and spirits with which we have been blessed. The following list offers some tips to aid you.

83

Hints to Aid You in Acquiring Healthy Habits

- Believe that you are able to change and improve your health
- Ask a friend or family member to serve as your coach so that you can have a buddy to offer support and hold you accountable
- Form mental images of the end result you want to achieve (e.g., a thinner body, a more relaxed state)
- Network with others who may be confronting similar challenges to share tips and offer support
- Keep a journal so that you can identify your progress, patterns, and pitfalls
- Use affirmations that describe the goals you will achieve ("I am able to eat a well-balanced diet, I am able to walk for 15 minutes every evening")
- Identify your accomplishments, reward yourself
- Pray for strength, patience, and perseverance to improve your health

This and the previous chapters have reviewed some of the basic elements of good health. However, knowledge alone won't get you there. Many people can recite what they ought to be doing to promote good health but that doesn't mean they're doing it. In the next chapter we'll examine some of the factors that can make or break your efforts to be healthy and what you need to do to get on a better path.

Study Questions

1. What messages about health are conveyed by society (e.g., through the media, advertisements, etc.)?

2. Why could people of faith be incorrect in assuming that their poor health condition is God's will?

3. What influence does physical and mental health have on your spiritual state?

4. How could a person who has a disease still be considered healthy?

5. What motivates individuals to promote unhealthy practices within their families?

6. How can you balance taking care of your health so that you can be a good steward of your body without preoccupation with physical health to the point of idolatry?

7. In what ways do sinful lifestyles contribute to health problems?

CHAPTER 5

Menopause 101

There is no typical menopause;
there are as many menopauses as women.
~Iris Murdoch~

As a cluster of my aunts and my mother's female friends sat around the kitchen table enjoying coffee and cheesecake, I noticed Aunt Margaret fanning herself vigorously as beads of perspiration rolled down her forehead. The room didn't seem warm and no one else was perspiring, but Aunt Margaret looked as though she was sitting in a steamroom.

"It looks like you're going through the change," said my grandmother teasingly.

"Yet another curse of women," responded Aunt Margaret with disgust.

"At least it's not causing you a nervous breakdown like it did Sophia down the street," chimed in one of the other women, triggering affirming nods from the group.

"What's *the change?*" I asked innocently.

"Go out and play with your friends, and don't put your nose in grown up affairs," ordered my mother.

I was all of eleven or twelve at the time but knew that whatever this change thing was, it must be something bad that grown up women dreaded and resented....and only talked about in private to other women.

That used to be the way menopause was handled. A mysterious change in a woman's life that was not well understood or discussed openly. For previous generations of women, preparation for menopause was even less adequate than preparation for menstruation and sex. Part of this had to do with prudishness that inhibited women from openly discussing bodily functions; some of it had to do with insufficient scientific understanding of menopausal changes and effective ways to manage them.

Times have changed. Research has provided greater insights into the changes that women's bodies experience at midlife and beyond. Gynecologists who once showed little interest in women past child-bearing years, are better equipped to help women address symptoms and reduce health risks that accompany this season of life. And today's women, in addition to being better informed and more assertive than their mothers' generation, also are more proactive in promoting optimal physical, mental, emotional, and sexual health as they age. It isn't their hot flashes that make them Women Afire, but rather their desire to live a full, active life until the day they die.

The Menstrual Cycle

As we examine the various actions that will enhance the ability of your body, mind, and spirit to be a Woman Afire, it may be helpful to have a realistic---and scientifically-based---understanding about menopause and its effects. We tend to think about our menstrual cycle as involving the organs below our waist, but this process actually begins in our brains. When the hypothalamus, a section of the brain that is concerned with regulating body functions detects that blood estrogen levels are low, it sends gonodotropin releasing hormone (GnRH) to the pituitary, a small gland located at the base of the brain. The pituitary gland responds by releasing follicle stimulating hormone (FSH) which stimulates the ovaries to produce estrogen and leutenizing hormone (LH) that is made available mid-cycle to cause ovulation.

Upon receiving their hormonal stimulation, the follicles in the ovaries release an egg. After the egg leaves the matured follicle, a small glandular mass is formed called the corpus luteum that manufactures the hormone progesterone. In addition to increasing the blood supply in the uterine lining to prepare for a possible pregnancy, progesterone has other important functions, such as helping with:

- the activity of thyroid hormone
- using fat for energy
- mood by serving as a natural antidepressant
- rest, calmness, and sleep through its sedating effect
- keeping blood sugar normal
- blood clotting
- libido
- preventing endometrial and ovarian cancer and ovarian cysts
- promoting bone strength by stimulating osteoblasts
- reducing arthritis symptoms by assisting with the production of cortisone
- eliminating fluids by acting as a diuretic

Like other hormones, progesterone can be measured in the blood, Blood values for progesterone range 0.2-0.8 ng/ml before ovulation and 2-26 ng/ml following ovulation.

If fertilization and implantation of the egg for pregnancy do not occur, estrogen and progesterone levels drop which causes a reduction in the blood supply to the tissues of the uterus. As the blood vessels constrict and relax, the unnourished endometrial layer of the uterus separates and dies. The shedding of this tissue is experienced as our monthly periods. At this time, estrogen levels are low which signals the hypothalamus to start the process all over again.

A woman is declared to be in **menopause** when menstrual periods have ceased for at least 12 consecutive months. The period of time 5-6 years before menopause, when hormonal levels are fluctuating widely, ovulation is inconsistent, and periods may be irregular is known as **perimenopause, menopause transition,** or **climacteric.** **Postmenopause** is the term used to mark the period after the last menstrual cycle (the first five postmenopausal years are considered early menopause and the time thereafter is late menopause). By age 40, most women begin skipping their periods. **Surgical menopause** is the removal of both ovaries prior to the onset of natural menopause and typically results in sudden, severe symptoms.

Many Hormones, Many Effects

Estrogen

Estrogen is an important hormone in our bodies that has several functions in addition influencing the production of eggs in our ovaries. Estrogen also:

- enhances blood flow to the brain
- promotes the growth of dendritic spines (structures on the nerve cell)
- increases the amount of an important chemical enzyme (choline acetyltransferase) that is needed to make acetylcholine, an important neurotransmitter (something that carries messages across our nerves) critical for memory
- regulates mood by enhancing the availability of the neurotransmitters serotonin, norepinephrine, and dopamine
- protects nerve cells from free-radical damage

In addition to being produced in the ovaries, estrogen is made in the adrenals (small glands behind the kidneys); it's also stored made in body fat which is the reason obese women may have higher estrogen levels than their thinner friends.

Women do produce different types of estrogen. **Estradiol** is the primary type produced prior to menopause. During perimenopause, **estrone**, produced in the ovaries and body fat, is the predominant type.

A glance at estrogen's functions offers insight into why we develop some of the symptoms associated with menopause. Symptoms of low estrogen levels are shown in the box that follows.

SYMPTOMS OF LOW ESTROGEN LEVELS

- hot flashes
- fatigue
- new onset of migraines
- heart palpitations, atypical angina
- restless leg
- vaginal dryness, itchiness
- insomnia
- decreased metabolic rate→weight gain
- increased fat on stomach and hips
- lower urinary tract symptoms: urinary frequency, stress incontinence, urgency, nighttime voiding
- symptoms of arthritis, fibromyalgia
- bladder and vaginal infections
- increased risk of osteoporosis, heart disease, colon cancer
- moodiness
- depression
- memory problems
- fuzzy/cloudy thinking
- inability to concentrate
- lower tolerance for annoyance
- greater impatience
- anxiety
- restlessness

During the years that we're menstruating, estradiol ranges 20-70 pg/ml before ovulation. There is a surge during ovulation to levels that exceed 200 pg/ml followed by a drop to 20-110 pg/ml after ovulation. Estradiol levels drop to 3-21 pg/ml after menopause. As menopause is approaching and estrogen levels begin to drop, higher levels of gonotropin-releasing hormone are released which in turn influences a higher production of FSH and LH. To complicate this matter further, follicles in the ovaries that haven't become depleted (a common occurrence in perimenopause) become resistant to FSH which could trigger a higher FSH production. These elevated levels can be detected through blood tests.

Progesterone

Progesterone falls in perimenopause but not in direct proportion to estrogen. A disproportionate amount of estrogen to progesterone is referred to as **estrogen dominance**. Some of the symptoms of estrogen dominance include breast swelling and tenderness, heavy irregular periods, water retention, cold hands and feet, and symptoms associated with PMS and menopause. (Be aware that phytoestrogens---the estrogens we obtain from plants and food---can increase this imbalance. We'll be reviewing that later.)

Testosterone

I recently attended a women's conference in which a speaker jokingly commented that "there isn't any testosterone in this auditorium." Actually, that's not a true statement because women do produce testosterone in their ovaries and adrenal glands. This hormone serves an important role in our interest and enjoyment of sex. The range of testosterone levels prior to menopause is 25-75 ng/dL. Testosterone declines by as much as 50% by midlife, resulting in reductions in sex drive, sensitivity to nipple stimulation, sexual arousal, and capacity for orgasm. The decline in this hormone also causes us to have less energy and to experience a thinning and loss of pubic hair. Blood tests can reveal reduced testosterone levels.

Thyroid Hormone

Thyroid hormone has significant functions in our bodies, too. It regulates the body's metabolism, therefore, altered levels of thyroid hormone can have profound and far-reaching effects. A conservative estimate is that by age 50, 20% of women have hypothyroidism---low thyroid function. This can cause symptoms that often mimic low estrogen levels, such as:

- weight gain
- breathing difficulties
- heavy periods
- low energy
- depression
- reduced immunity
- muscle weakness
- fibromyalgia
- constipation
- memory problems
- night sweats
- sleep disturbances
- dry skin and hair
- low body temperature
- intolerance to cold
- decreased libido

When thyroid levels in the blood are low, a greater amount of thyroid stimulating hormone (TSH) is produced which is one way that this change can be detected through blood tests. (Other blood tests of thyroid function include measurements of levels of thyroxine, triodothyonine, and thyroid antibodies.) Although there is a relationship between the decline of estrogen and thyroid hormones with age, at this point the way in which a reduction in one influences a reduction in the other is uncertain. Estrogen dominance can block the action of thyroid hormone.

The adrenals, those small glands mentioned earlier, have an effect on the various hormones in our body. This is a consideration in regard to stress management as stress can affect the function of the adrenals leading to hormonal imbalances. Reduced adrenal function is characterized by:

- moodiness
- muscle weakness
- allergies
- low energy, particularly during late afternoon
- not feeling refreshed when waking

Although menopause is thought to be associated with a reduction in estrogen and progesterone, you can see that menopause is a much more complicated hormonal process than that. Reliable testing of hormonal levels is done through analysis of blood or saliva.

Managing Menopause Symptoms

We live in a society that has a remarkable medical system that has unraveled the most intricate workings of the human body and developed medications, surgical procedures, and therapies to address most conditions. You could assume, then, that sound knowledge about the management of menopause symptoms would have existed for some time---especially as unlike common health conditions, menopause is something that affects every woman who reaches midlife and beyond. Your assumption would be wrong.

Hormone therapy for the treatment of menopausal symptoms has a long history that, unfortunately, was marked by prescribing the use of hormones before the full effects were known. Estrogen began being used for menopausal symptoms in the 1940s when it was discovered that it could be extracted from the urine of pregnant mares. Not many women used estrogen, initially, but that changed in the mid-60s when books and articles promoted estrogen therapy as a means to cure just about every ill of aging. The first shoe, along with estrogen use, dropped in the 1970s when studies revealed that postmenopausal women with an intact uterus who used estrogen had higher rates of endometrial cancer. New studies then suggested that endometrial cancer risk was removed if estrogen was combined with progestogen (progesterone and progestin). Until the turn of the century the practice of prescribing estrogen and progestogen for women with a uterus and estrogen alone for women without a uterus continued.

The other shoe began a steady, profound drop in 2002 when the results of the Women's Health Initiative (WHI) became available.

The Women's Health Initiative was launched in 1991 by the National Institutes of Health and the National Heart, Lung, and Blood Institute to study the major health issues facing postmenopausal women. It included research into the use of hormones: estrogen alone and estrogen plus progestin.

The estrogen plus progestin study was discontinued earlier than planned because it was apparent that the risks of the therapy outweighed the benefits. While colorectal cancer and fracture rates were lower, cardiovascular disease and invasive breast cancer rates were higher.

The estrogen-alone study also was stopped earlier than planned. The study intended to show that estrogen therapy reduced the risk of cardiovascular disease. Although the rates of invasive breast cancer and fractures were lower, there was no significant cardiovascular benefit and there was a hint that the risk for stroke increased.

> The study also looked at the effects of hormone therapy on memory. The results were inconclusive.
>
> Needless to say, the study created much controversy and discussion.

The current recommendations are that:

- estrogen can be used to treat menopausal symptoms but should be prescribed at the *lowest effective dosage for the shortest period of time*
  - o it should be used only for the treatment of moderate to severe symptoms and for the prevention of osteoporosis (the benefits in preventing osteoporosis are lost when the hormone is no longer used)
  - o it should not be used by women with breast cancer, a history of breast cancer, suspected or known estrogen-sensitive cancers, coronary artery disease, untreated hypertension, active liver disease, pulmonary embolism, undiagnosed vaginal bleeding, or high sensitivity to hormone therapy
- women with a uterus should have progestogen prescribed with the estrogen to counteract the increased risk of endometrial cancer
- women without a uterus should not use progestogen
- women 60 and older who have never taken hormone therapy shouldn't start unless there is a strong reason to do so; these women need to be monitored closely by their physicians for cardiovascular risks
- when estrogen is used only to treat vaginal symptoms, local administration rather than oral is recommended

- hormone therapy should not be used for the prevention of cardio-vascular conditions, dementia, depression, or other chronic diseases

The use of bioidentical custom-compounded hormones is not recommended. There is no scientific evidence that they, and many of the herbal and other "natural" products to address menopause symptoms are safer or more effective than conventional hormone therapy. (See Table 4 in the Appendix for a description of these therapies.) Although many of the herbs recommended for the management of menopausal symptoms lack scientific evidence, a standardized extract of rhapontic rhubarb (*Rheum rhaponticum*) has been shown through a placebo-controlled study to significantly reduce hot flashes and other symptoms of menopause (Geller, 2009).

Although there are some basic similarities in symptoms and changes, menopause is a unique journey for every woman. Health condition and risks, family history, goals, and personal preferences are among the factors that support individualized approaches. Some of the complementary therapies, such as mind-body and acupuncture, could offer some relief while carrying minimal risk.

The following websites can be visited for current, scientifically-based information about treatment options for menopause symptoms:

National Cancer Institute

www.cancer.gov/clinicaltrials/digest-postmenopausal-hormone-use

National Institutes of Health

http://health.nih.gov/topic/Menopause

North American Menopause Society

www.menopause.org

Women's Health Initiative

www.nhlbi.nih.gov/whi

It's Not Just Your Experience

Menopause does not occur in a vacuum. Granted, the physical changes to a woman's reproductive system affect her individual body; however, the meaning and value culture assigns to this landmark have significant implications. For instance, in the Victorian era, "moral insanity" was associated with menopause. A physician of the time described the view well when he noted (Tilt, 1882):

> *During the change of life the nervous system is so unhinged that the management of the mental and moral faculties often taxes the ingenuity of the medical confidant....(the disturbance) can cause normally moral women to act without principle...be untruthful...be peevish...even have fits of temper...steal...leave their families...brood in melancholy self absorption.*

Engaging in sexual intercourse, dancing, reading novels, and showing anger were believed to excite the nervous system and endanger the health of the woman during this change. Women were encouraged to withdraw from activities outside the home and live a calm existence, focused primarily on domestic affairs.

Women no longer are viewed solely on the basis of their childbearing and domestic capabilities. Today's woman has a wide range of roles and choices available. However, although having sex, dancing, reading novels, and displaying anger are no longer viewed as hazardous to a woman's health at menopause and beyond, there still are too few examples of mature women who are considered sexy, free-spirited, and powerful.

Today's women are carving out new paths for their lives at menopause and beyond. Armed with greater scientific insights into healthy aging and the management of menopause symptoms, women can enter the later seasons of their lives with sound physical and mental health. This, combined with fewer misconceptions, prejudices, and stereotypes about mature women, frees women to fill diverse roles and unleash powerful influence. Both women and the society in which they live will be enriched by an enlightened understanding of menopause.

Reference

Geller, S. (2009). Improving the science for botanical and dietary supplements. Alternative Therapies in Health and Medicine, 15(1):16-17.

Tilt, E.J. (1882). The Change of Life in Health and Disease. A Clinical Treatise on the Diseases of the Ganglionic Nervous System Incidental to Women at the Decline of Life. New York: Bermingham, p. 101.

Study Questions

1. What has been your pattern of symptoms with menstrual periods, perimenopause and/or menopause? What have you found to affect these symptoms---positively and negatively?
2. Currently, what are you doing to improve or worsen your symptoms?
3. How would you compare menopause as a *season* of life?
4. What do you recall the older women in your family saying about menopause? What do you think influenced their thinking?

CHAPTER 6

Nurturing Yourself

The way we live our days,
is the way we live our lives.
~Annie Dillard~

When you think of the word nurture you may associate it with investing in your children so they realize their potential or nourishing a garden so it is abundant with flowers and fruits. The nurturing efforts put into young lives and gardens are proactive actions to yield positive results. Likewise, *self-nurturing* is an essential part of a healthy, balanced life.

Spiritual Disciplines

The spiritual disciplines provide a solid framework for self-nurturing. Spiritual disciplines are activities intentionally engaged in that enliven and deepen your relationship to God. Important aspects to understand are that they are *intentional*, that is, done purposefully rather than by chance, and are *focused on God*. An abundant, balanced life demands interaction with a living, personal God that is intentional rather than haphazard. Regular practice of the spiritual disciplines helps you to tap into God's power. Spiritual disciplines enable you to deepen your understanding and relationship to yourself, as well, to help you to unpeel layers of your composition and understand your core. The result is an achievement of a more abundant life---a deeper life in the spirit.

There are a variety of activities that are regarded as spiritual disciplines. Richard Foster (2009) identifies the spiritual disciplines as:

Inward Disciplines: meditation, prayer, fasting, study

Outward Disciplines: simplicity, solitude, submission, service

Corporate Disciplines: confession, worship, guidance, celebration

Dallas Willard (1990, 2009), takes a different approach to categorizing the spiritual disciplines by dividing them into disciplines that disengage us from those life activities that interfere with our relationship with God (Disciplines of Abstinence) and disciplines that immerse us more deeply in God's kingdom (Disciplines of Engagement); his lists include:

Disciplines of Abstinence: solitude, silence, fasting, frugality, chastity, secrecy, sacrifice, watching

Disciplines of Engagement: study, worship, celebration, service, prayer, fellowship, confession, submission

There is nothing mysterious about the practice of spiritual disciplines. The Bible offers fine examples of how Jesus and His disciples wove these practices into their routine lives and instructed others to do so as part of the Christian life. For example:

After He had dismissed them, He went up on a mountainside by Himself to pray. .. *Matthew 14:23*

Therefore, confess your sins to each other and pray for each other so that you may be healed. *James 5:16*

Let us not give up meeting together... *Hebrews 10:25*

Jesus stopped and called them, "What do you want me to do for you?" He asked. *Matthew 21:32*

...and whoever wants to be first must be your slave---just as the Son of Man did not come to be served, but to serve... *Matthew 20:27*

But Jesus often withdrew to lonely places and prayed... *Luke 5:16*

Great musicians didn't first pick up their instruments and begin playing in a symphony orchestra. World Series baseball players didn't progress from Little League to Major League overnight. Skilled cardiac surgeons didn't take scalpels to people's chests on their first day in medical school. The ease and expertise demonstrated by individuals who have achieved greatness in their fields have come from considerable focus, study, and practice. The behaviors that now seem to come easily and naturally to these talented persons are the result of a considerable investment of time and effort. They ate, slept, and breathed the talent they desired to master. Likewise, your regular focus, study, and practice of the spiritual disciplines can lead you to an abundant, meaningful life.

Prayer

Of all the spiritual disciplines, prayer is the one that probably is most commonly practiced. This communication with God enlivens one's faith and nurtures the soul. Although discussed in an earlier chapter, prayer warrants some further attention here.

As simple as it seems, prayer risks being misunderstood. I recall one of my early experiences in learning to pray---or at least that is what it was labeled. I was somewhere in the neighborhood of 12 years of age and attending a Greek Orthodox church. At that time, the full service was spoken in Greek; unfortunately, I neither spoke nor understood Greek. However, my Sunday school assignment was to learn the Apostle's Creed---in Greek! My anxiety brewed. How was I ever going to do this? I imagined the embarrassment at being the only one among my peers---all of whom were quite fluent in Greek by the way---unable to recite the words. My Sunday school teacher, sensitive to my plight, volunteered to tutor me in the task. For several weeks, nearly every evening, this dedicated woman taught me verse after verse, phonetically. I'd practice in front of my parents, in front of the mirror, in front of my dog, in front of anything that would stay still long enough to hear me recite in a foreign tongue. When the time came for me to stand before my class and recite the Creed, I was able to do so. In fact, I was so impressive that I was selected to recite the Apostle's Creed at the assembly for parents. My head swelled from the compliments I received in my delivery of this prayer. It wasn't until I reached adulthood that I actually read the Creed in English and understood what I had been saying.

My parroting of foreign words could hardly be considered praying. Yet, reciting prayers by rote is no more effective a means of prayer either, despite the fact that it is done in one's own language. Prayer isn't about spurting out impressive sounding scripture but *communicating with God.* There are many fine books that offer guidance on the process of prayer; however, the basic instructions have been provided by the greatest spiritual teacher of all, Jesus Christ. He instructed his disciples (Matthew 6: 5-13) to pray:

- privately to God without great show or fanfare
- simply and clearly, avoiding unnecessary wordiness and babbling

106

- with offerings of praise to God
- for the advancement of God's kingdom in this world
- for the provision of daily needs, recognizing that God best knows those needs
- for forgiveness and with a heart to forgive others
- for strength to recognize and resist temptation
- with acknowledgement that God is the ultimate power in all lives

There needn't be formality in prayer, but rather, a normal conversational style as though communicating with a friend. God is not concerned with your eloquence but that you are coming to Him. You can compare it to the way parents feel when their children come to them with an honest, open expression of feelings and concerns. The parents are touched by their children's heart, not the sophistication of their communication style, and delight in the fact that their children love and trust them sufficiently to seek their advice and assistance. So too, God delights when His children seek his guidance and help.

There can be a variety of intents to your prayer. Prayers of *thanksgiving* offer praise to God for His creation, presence, and actions. Prayers of *intercession* enable you to express your love for others---your family members, ministers, missionaries, government leaders, warring nations, the troubled-looking teen behind the counter at the fast-food restaurant---by lifting their needs to God. Prayers for *healing* show your faith that God can bring comfort, peace, and purpose in the midst of physical and emotional suffering. Prayers for *forgiveness* of your sin helps you to maintain a short account with God and clears the path from obstacles that could interfere with the experience of spiritual peace and fulfillment. Prayers for God's *guidance* reflect your dependence on Him for the decisions and actions facing you as you live your life.

Meditating on Scripture as part of prayer can deepen communication with God and offer profound insights. It is remarkable how God can speak if you take the time to listen.

Leanne Payne in her book *Listening Prayer* (2000) describes practices that hinder prayer. She cautions against the "disease of introspection" that causes us to sink into self-analysis during prayer time whereby we focus on ourselves rather than God. Substitution is another hindrance and occurs when we pray to take on another person's pain or troubles, thereby becoming the savior-redeemer rather than allowing God to assume His rightful role. Focusing on fighting demons and praying against Satan also hinders prayer as it distracts us from the focus of our prayers---God.

It is useful for you to dedicate a specific time of day for prayer. Like any other practice, establishing a routine increases the likelihood that prayer becomes a habit. In addition, you can engage in short prayer throughout the day. These short prayers can relate to issues included in your routine prayer time or issues that surface as you go about your daily activities. For example, you may pray that:

- you be helped to show patience and grace with the less than polite drivers on the highway
- you adopt a servant's heart rather than complain about the dishes left in the sink
- you be guided to make the best decision regarding how to respond to an invitation from a neighbor who you think you have nothing in common with
- the person in the ambulance that passes you receives the care needed in a timely manner

Your deep, routine prayers help to knit a strong fabric of relationship with God that covers you as you face life's challenges. In addition, your short incidental prayers provide patches that reinforce the areas of life subjected to greater stress and prevent frayed fragments from tearing apart the basic fabric of a faithful life.

Study

My father became employed as a bricklayer for Bethlehem Steel Company after his discharge from the Navy. He had intentions of working there long enough to accumulate some money and return to college. A growing family and pay incentives diverted his plans, and he spent the next 41 years lining brick walls inside blast furnaces. The basic bricklaying skills he learned as an apprentice were sufficient to guide his career, and he was not required nor did he care to attend continuing education courses or read books about bricklaying. There was only so much one could learn about bricks and mortar.

A full, dynamic life is not repetition of the same experience. Rather, it requires that you be a lifelong student. There are many fine books that can be used for study. A visit to your local or online bookstore can reveal the variety of topics to explore, such as classical writings, contemporary issues, and guides for parenting, marriage, dating, and other aspects of living.

Group study can provide rich opportunities for learning. Many churches offer Bible studies classes. BSF (Bible Study Fellowship International) is an interdenominational lay organization that offers classes throughout the world for men, women, and children; for the location in your community you may visit their website at www.bsfinternational.org or call 1-877-273-3228. In addition, there are many easy-to-use study guides and books that include study questions that can be used to lead a group study.

Retreats can complement regular study and provide an intense study time. Free from daily distractions, you may find you are able to concentrate more fully and spend longer blocks of time in uninterrupted contemplation. In addition to retreats sponsored by groups, you also can schedule your own private retreat. I know of mothers of young children who exchange weekend babysitting so that each one can enjoy a retreat while knowing their children are being well-cared for---and without burdening the family budget. My husband and I combine some of our vacation time together with private retreat periods by staying at a site that provides outdoor areas or space within the hotel where we can get away from each other for blocks of time; after a full day of solitude and study, we reconnect for the evening. Think creatively as to the model that can work for you.

Self-study is a valuable exercise. It can be quite beneficial to periodically take stock of your life---your habits, your concerns, your reactions, burdens---and the people or events that influence you. Consider factors that could be contributing to your problems. You may find the core issues are that you are not in touch with your spiritual dimension

Being attentive to the world around you is another important aspect of study. Allow your senses to study and experience the beauty of creation---the soft layers of feathers on a bird, the delicate petals on a flower, the scent of newly mowed grass, the sensation of raindrops against your face. Study the people around you to see how their lives are moving and lessons you can learn from them. Study the culture also. There is a risk that you may become so entwined in your immediate circle---primarily socializing with friends from your neighborhood, listening to the same type of music, reading the same type of literature---that you are not aware of the activities and trends within society that could impact you and your family.

Worship

In the broadest sense, to worship is to adore God and honor His worth. Most of us tend to think of religious services within church buildings or synagogues as worship, however, our praise, adoration, and celebration of God ideally are integrated into our daily lives if we are women of faith---not just reserved for the Sabbath. We worship God when we acknowledge that He is the creator of the sweet song the bird sings outside our window; when we treat the stranger we encounter in the mall with sensitivity and respect; when we take a pause from our daily routines to feel, *truly feel,* deep gratitude for the blessings of our lives; and when we open our hearts and minds and invite God to speak to us.

An exciting connection with God and others can be achieved through the corporate worship experience. People who gather with the expectancy of dynamic interaction with God create a sacred space that allows God to be present. The unity of multiple spirits has a synergy that surpasses the power of a single individual. Together they sing, pray, dance, and rejoice to praise him. Their whole bodies engage with God; their hearts and spirits are naked before Him.

It is important for you to find a house of worship in which you can achieve a sense of community. It should be a place in which you can connect with others, comfortably participate, and focus on the worship experience. This may mean that it may not be the most convenient or elaborate building, but is one that facilitates a dynamic, interactive relationship with God. It isn't the building that houses the worshipers that is important, but rather, the worship experience that is housed within the structure.

Fasting

Although discussed earlier in the context of health habits, it is beneficial to reinforce the importance of fasting. Secular health advocates promote the health benefits of fasting, yet people of faith need to remember that fasting has been a spiritual discipline for as far back as can be remembered.

You may think of fasting in terms of the omission of food; however, fasting from certain behaviors also must be considered. In her personal journals, Catherine Marshall (1986), a gifted storyteller and wife of a former U. S. Senate Chaplain, describes how she attempted to fast from having a critical spirit for one day. This proved to be a challenge as she came to understand how automatic this behavior had become. During the day of fasting from critical behavior, she gained insight into the fruitlessness of her ways and the extent to which it had blocked relationships and creativity. Convicted of her behavior, she was able to seek forgiveness and seek a new path. Be it criticism, sarcasm, nagging, gossiping, or other behaviors that separate us from positive, full relationships with God and others, fasting from sinful behaviors can aid in breaking our chains to them.

Fasting helps to keep balance in your life and prevents nonessential food, activities, stimulation, and other temptations from diverting your focus from spiritual matters. The space that is left empty as a result of the fast can be filled by a divine presence. Dallas Willard puts it well when he says "In fasting, we learn how to suffer happily as we feast on God."

Meditation

Meditation can be a challenging discipline to practice because we live in a society that encourages and rewards us for our *doing* rather than our *being.* Multitasking…improving efficiency and productivity… high-speed internet. We constantly are bombarded with messages on how we can do more, faster. In the midst of this climate, the act of sitting still and "doing nothing" can seem like a waste of time. Yet, this act can be critical to helping us to define ourselves by authentic standards, not the world's, and enabling us to explore our spiritual dimensions.

Although it is the substance not the mechanics of meditation that is important, there are some factors that can enhance the experience:

- Find a quiet, peaceful setting. Some people find that sitting in a garden or near a body of water facilitates meditation. However, if you don't have access to peaceful natural settings, you can create your own "sacred space" for meditating by placing some potted plants, candles, and religious objects on a table and instilling scents (aromatherapy) in the room. Peaceful background music can be beneficial, also.
- Sit in a comfortable position; a lotus pose is not essential but sitting can be superior to lying down to assure you don't drift to sleep.
- Close your eyes and breathe deeply. As you inhale, think about bringing in the light and love of God or a Higher Power; as you exhale release those thoughts that trouble or tempt you.
- Think about an attribute of someone whose life is exemplary, a relevant quote, Scripture verse, a recent experience in which you saw God work in your life.
- Be still and attentive to messages that you may receive or insights that you may gain.
- If distractions (telephones, doorbells) or thoughts (I forgot to pick up milk, I wonder if the kids made a mess) invade your experience, take a deep breath and reorient yourself to meditating.

Some people find journaling after meditating useful to record insights gained.

The act of meditation can promote the development of a meditative state of mind---i.e., being present in the moment---that permeates even the most common aspects of your daily life. You can become more attuned to the here and now, and control the extent to which distractions divert your attention. You can notice life's gifts in a renewed way. Examples of simple exercises to increase the art of being present in the moment include:

- Place a raisin in your palm. Examine all the ridges, the shape, the color of the fruit. Roll it between your fingers and feel the texture. Smell the raisin and then place it on your tongue. Roll it on your tongue, feeling the texture and size. Slowly chew the raisin and taste its flavor.
- Find a leaf that has fallen to the ground or pick one from a tree. Examine the color and shape, noticing changes from one section of the leaf to another. Gently stroke both sides of the leaf. Crush it in your hand and be aware of the feeling. Hold the pieces of the leaf to your nose and detect any scent that is present. Toss the pieces of the leaf in the air and watch them settle to the ground.

Simple acts such as these can help you to become more sensitive to the beauty and complexity of the earth. The development of a meditative state of mind can help you to stay in touch with your spiritual side throughout your daily routines, still your racing mind so that you keep stress under control, and maintain balance in your life.

Some Christians are reluctant to meditate because the commonly promoted model of Eastern or transcendental meditation that encourages deep relaxation with an emptying of the mind, promotes a state of altered consciousness that potentially enables one to communicate with spiritual guides and be open to spiritual influences that could be demonic. But, there is a place for meditation in the lives of Christians, and it is an important discipline. In fact, the Bible shows evidence of this practice:

He (Isaac) went out to the field one evening to meditate Genesis 24:63

Do not let this Book of the Law depart from your mouth; meditate on it day and night... Joshua 1:8

But his delight is in the law of the Lord, and on his law he meditates day and night Psalm 1:2

My eyes stay open through the watches of the night, that I may meditate on your promises. Psalm 119:148

...we take captive every thought to make it obedient to Christ 2 Corinthians10:5

There certainly are health benefits associated when people of faith meditate, but most important is the closer relationship with God that can result. Meditation as a spiritual discipline doesn't empty the mind but rather, focuses it on God and everything about Him. When the mind is quieted, we often are able to gain insights from God and achieve greater union with Him.

Solitude

Solitude was discussed earlier as a means to manage stress. Like meditation, this practice, although having health benefits, most importantly is a spiritual discipline that deepens our connection to our spiritual selves.

In addition to periods of solitude (e.g., several days away), you can also find mini-opportunities to practice this discipline by refraining from speech and interaction during the day. I know that personally, it is difficult for me to arrange a weekly day of solitude; however, I do find that I can build some solitude into each day by my habit of rising early and using that early morning time to read devotionals and pray. You may find that you can schedule a short break between your arrival home and the beginning of household responsibilities to retreat to a corner of your home where your privacy will be respected, and you can have some quiet time. You can achieve a state of solitude while sitting in traffic or on a bus as you block out the hustle-bustle around you and reflect on God and His creation. Although it is ideal to have a physical space where you can be alone for a period of time, when this is not possible, you can create a psychological and spiritual space to achieve inner peace wherever you are.

Self-Love

You must love yourself in order to understand how to love others. One of the obstacles to the ability to fully love yourself could rest in the emotional baggage you carry regarding your shortcomings, failures, and sin. Consider Marcie's example:

> *Ten years ago, while on a business trip, Marcie and a few of her associates decided to meet in the hotel lounge for a few drinks to celebrate the closing of a contract. After several rounds of drinks, Marcie spotted what she believed to be the most handsome man she had seen in a long time sitting at a table with some other men. Although married, Marcie's inhibitions were significantly relaxed as a result of the alcohol. She was flattered when this object of her attention asked her to dance. After a little playful objection, she conceded.*
> *Marcie learned that the man's name was Eric and that he was married with two small children. Marcie and Eric shared several more dances and drinks, and began to confide how their marriages were unfulfilling. Before they knew it they exchanged a kiss, and then*

proceeded to Eric's hotel room where they both experienced their first affair.

The following morning, Marcie's sense of excitement over-came the feelings of guilt she felt about her transgression. She believed she experienced things she hadn't felt in a long time. "This man is my soulmate," she thought. "I've got to be with him."

The next several months were a whirlwind of rendezvous. The two met every chance they could. It was as though Marcie wore special lenses that highlighted all the wonderful things about Eric while exaggerating every fault of her husband. Less than four months after meeting, Marcie and Eric left their spouses and moved in together, over the objections and pleadings of their respective families.

This was the boldest things Marcie had ever done in her life. She was usually responsible and level-headed, but threw reason to the wind and followed her feelings. Her husband had suspected nothing and was shocked that the life to which he was committed was crum-bling before him. Marcie still remembers the sick feeling in her stomach as her husband packed his things in his car, sobbing uncontrollably, with their little boy screaming, "Daddy, don't go." Although she had some thoughts that perhaps she was making a mistake, Marcie knew Eric had left his wife to be with her and felt that she had gone too far to turn back now.

The first year after leaving her husband was almost surreal. The worlds Marcie and Eric had known were destroyed as few friends and family associated with them. Eric's children were acting out due to having their lives uprooted. Marcie's son rejected Eric and cried for his dad's return. Financial pressures mounted as Eric faced responsibility for two families.

Marcie sensed some yellow lights in her relationship with Eric, but ignored them, believing things would work out and that she had to accept her lot. Despite knowing problems existed in the relationship, Marcie married Eric as soon as their divorces were final. Within a year Marcie was pregnant. Eric was resentful as he trusted Marcie to faithfully use birth control. "The last thing I need are more expenses," he thought. Shortly after their first child together was born, they had a second, then a third child.

What had once been an exciting, passionate relationship now was burdensome and stressful. There never seemed to be enough money and Marcie never seemed to miss an opportunity to remind Eric of this, particularly as her first husband had become extremely successful in his business. The couple's sexual relationship felt more like an act of duty than an act of love. The kids complained that they couldn't afford the same things as their friends. Eric's children from his first marriage resented that they got less of their father's attention and resources than their father's new family.

Marcie began to feel that she was reaping the results of her sin. She had committed adultery, caused the break-up of two families, hurt innocent people, made a mess of many lives. She reacted by withdrawing and becoming hostile. The slightest mishap or comment could set off a violent reaction that caused her to be verbally abusive to anyone in her path. In the valley of self-hatred in which she lived, Marcie could not truly love others.

There is no ignoring the reality that Marcie betrayed her wedding vows; her adultery was wrong. Further, choosing the path of compounding her wrongs instead of repenting and returning to a right path increased her troubles. Imagine how differently Marcie's life could have unfolded if after that first night in the hotel she had confessed her actions to her husband and God; asked both of them for forgiveness; asked Eric for forgiveness; urged Eric to set things right with his wife and God; sought counseling; and prayed for guidance and strength.

Every one of us makes mistakes, hurts others, does some very stupid things. This is part of being human. Feeling badly and sorry about these behaviors is understandable. But, we need to move beyond those feelings. We start by having a repentant heart, reflecting, and gaining insight so that we can learn and avoid similar actions in the future. We then need to forgive ourselves, as we would forgive a loved one who made a similar mistake, learned from it, and repented. Showing ourselves the same forgiveness, grace, and mercy that we would show others demonstrates self-love.

References

Foster, R. Celebration of Discipline, 2d ed, San Francisco: Harper Collins, 2009.

Marshall, C. A Closer Walk. Old Tappan, NJ: Chosen Books/Revell, 1986.

Payne, L. Listening Prayer. Learning to Hear God's Voice and Keep a Prayer Journal, Grand Rapids, MI: Baker Books, 2000, p58-59.

Willard, D. The Divine Conspiracy: Rediscovering Our Hidden Life in God, San Francisco: HarperSanFrancisco, 1998, p418.

Willard, D. The Spirit of the Disciplines. Understanding How God Changes Lives, San Francisco: HarperSanFrancisco, 1990, p. 167. Kindle edition 2009.

Study Questions

1. What are some obstacles to meditation? How can they be overcome?

2. What are some of the pros and cons of "studying" secular behaviors and trends?

3. Which of the spiritual disciplines discussed in this chapter are particularly challenging for you to practice? Why? What can you do to increase their presence in your life?

4. What unresolved sins or wrongs of your past prevent you from loving yourself? How can you relieve this burden?

CHAPTER 7

Navigating Life Transitions

*Change is the law of life and those who look only to the past or present
are certain to miss the future.*
~John F. Kennedy~

Today's woman who is at midlife or beyond typically faces many more opportunities and changes than did her mother and grandmother. In addition to living longer and, therefore, having more time for issues to emerge, she is more likely than previous generations of women to be dealing with adult children who return to or never leave the nest, parent care, divorce, remarriage, return to the labor force, career changes, body image concerns, and helping her own children raise their children as single parents.

Fortunately, today's generation of women who are 50 and older have witnessed and experienced many significant transitions during their lifetimes, such as:

- the feminist movement which empowered and opened doors for women
- the Pill which provided new reproductive options
- the acceptance of women in competitive sports
- a greater acceptance of women in careers that once were predominately male (e.g., law, medicine)

Having been a generation who has weathered such storms of change, today's mature women may be better equipped than their ancestors to successfully navigate and chart new territory with life transitions as they face mid and late life.

Factors Influencing Change

As have been discussed in previous chapters, there are a variety of internal changes that affect women at midlife and beyond, such as the those accompanying menopause and normal aging. In addition, a woman may find that the people, interests, and activities in her life have changed, sometimes causing her to view them as boring or unsatisfying. There can be a desire to challenge oneself with something new and to engage in something that has meaning. At this stage of life, a woman may question the decisions she has made, such as forfeiting a career to be a homemaker or forfeiting time with her family to pursue a career. She may reach her 60s and feel that she doesn't really want to be spend her limited time and energy on a job that she really doesn't need, yet have no idea what she will do to fill her days if she should live another 30 years. Questions about the meaning of life can emerge, leading to anxiety, depression, and confusion.

In addition to internal factors, external ones can cause changes and uncomfortable feelings. Television commercials featuring older adults who are facing financial hurdles, articles that outline how much one should have invested for retirement, and invitations in the mail to attend financial planning seminars can stir concern over one's financial security. There may be awareness that the years of accruing debt, being generous with offspring, and not hesitating to pull out the credit card can't continue. Subtle (and perhaps, not so subtle) messages communicated in the workplace may lead one to question if the demands of the job can still be met. Grief and readjustments increasingly may be confronted as changes in relationships through death, divorce, and illness become more common.

The transitions faced at this stage of life can present a crisis or an opportunity. The emptiness of children grown and gone can be replaced by new interests and friendships. With college expenses out of the way, mortgages paid, and job tenure producing a decent income for herself and/or her spouse, the woman may have greater financial resources at her disposal. Sex may be enjoyed in a renewed way with the threat of pregnancy eliminated and children out of the house. A repressed or new identity may emerge that can prove to be exciting and rewarding. The successful management of transitions can result in a life that highly satisfying and purposeful.

Marriage

The marriage relationship is a very special and sacred one. It also can be among the more challenging of the relationships experienced, particularly in the 21st Century when the message from the secular world implies that the Biblical model for a marital relationship is irrelevant and even oppressive. Same sex marriages and parenting increasingly are accepted as legitimate options to the traditional nuclear family model. In some circles, the concept of wives submitting to husbands as head of the family is viewed as highly distasteful and demeaning to women. Celebrities who birth babies out of wedlock are glamorized while the couple who commits to traditional principles of childrearing get little recognition.

I must confess to sharing society's critical views of marriage throughout most of my adult life, before becoming a Christian. I entered adulthood during the rise of feminism when "women can have it all" seemed to be the mantra. The stay-at-home mom families I had seen often reflected women frustrated by boredom and underutilized gifts, and husbands who ran the extremes of abusive tyrants to detached paycheck providers. Marriage was fine as long as everyone *felt good* within it; if it was no longer fulfilling or if a better opportunity caught one's eye, a marriage could be broken and one could move on to greener pastures. Despite tracking in many circles and having many friends and acquaintances, no one ever shared the Biblical model for marriage. It wasn't until midlife that I learned about God's plan for marriage and the blessings it held. I can't help but wonder if many other people are misguided because people of faith haven't come into their paths and boldly shared the realities and virtues of Biblical manhood and womanhood.

So, what does the Bible tell us about marriage?

- God created man and woman to be in relationship and multiply (Genesis 1:27-28; 2:18). He could have chosen to let Adam rule alone or to provide a same sex partner to rule with Adam, yet God created two different sexed beings to complement each other and reproduce.
- Marriage is a sacred act that is a dynamic reflection of Christ and the Church (Ephesians 5:23-33).
- Being created in the image of God, both sexes are equal in worth (Genesis 1:26; 1 Peter 2:17).

- The husband is the head of his wife (Genesis 2:15-25; Ephesians 5:22-33; 1Corinthians 11:3). This headship does not imply male dominance, but rather, the husband leading, protecting and loving his wife as Christ did in his authority over the Church.
- The wife is to submit to her husband and be his helpmate (Genesis 2:18; Ephesians 5:22-33; 1Corinthians 11:3). This does not suggest that the woman is inferior to the man, but that they have distinctly different and complementary roles within the family. It is interesting to note that in the Hebrew text, helper does not imply subordination but usually is used in context of God helping and serving others.
- Marriage is intended to be lasting (Matthew 19:6). Jesus made it clear that He did not condone finding reasons to divorce, but in committing to a lasting relationship.
- Marriage is to be filled with joy, romance, and intimacy, as a creation of God (Song of Songs).

It is no secret that God's principles for a holy marriage cause interesting reactions in society that often can create challenges for persons of faith. Audrey's example is a case in point.

Audrey and Bill met in high school and experienced an immediate attraction. Despite attending colleges in different states, their relationship deepened. They both were committed Christians and shared similar values.

Following college graduation they married. They both continued their education while working part-time and in a few years, Bill became a CPA and Audrey obtained a law degree and passed the bar. A bright and dynamic couple, they supported each other's careers.

125

After a few years of marriage, the couple was blessed with a daughter. Audrey had stopped working during her last month of pregnancy and stayed at home with her child until she entered first grade. At that time, with her husband's enthusiastic support, Audrey decided to return to work, part-time. The stimulation was welcomed, as was the extra money that came in handy for her daughter's private school. She was able to take cases that afforded her a schedule that allowed her to be home when her daughter left and returned from school; however, even with a part-time schedule she found it challenging to cook homemade meals and keep a tidy house. Bill pitched in as he could, but the housekeeping standards within their home were considerably more relaxed than before she returned to work.

It didn't take long for Audrey to begin feeling that she fit into neither the professional world nor the mommy world. Colleagues would question how she could let her investment in her career be under-utilized by taking "Mickey Mouse cases" and not participating in activities for professional advancement. Her stay-at-home friends would ask her if she felt her family was suffering because her time and energy were being shared with a job; there was an implication that working outside the home was improper for a Christian wife and mother. Audrey began to feel that she was a foreigner in both lands, and even worse, that perhaps she was being an ungodly wife and mother.

Audrey's dilemma is not an uncommon one. Many feminists would balk at a woman forfeiting her career to stay at home to care for husband, home, and children. And on the other hand, there are people of faith who would criticize a woman who chose to work outside the home. Certainly, a mother's presence with a child during the early years of life is significant to the child's optimal development; no day care arrangement is superior to the nurturing provided by a loving parent. Attending to the physical, emotional, and spiritual well-being of one's child is a demonstration of good stewardship of this blessing from God. However, God has not forbid women from having gainful employment outside the home. In fact, a review of the attributes of the Proverbs 31 Wife of Noble Character demonstrates this in that she (Proverbs 31:10-31):

- works with eager hands
- brings food from afar
- provides food for her family
- considers a field, buys it, and works it
- sets about her work vigorously
- sees that her trading is profitable
- makes and sells linen garments
- watches over the affairs of her household
- does not eat the bread of idleness

Couples at midlife often need to clarify values, roles, and expectations. Particularly in couples who were married decades earlier, relationship dynamics may need to be explored and redefined based on the mature individuals they have become (that may bear little resemblance to the naive kids who said "I do"). This need to learn about each other as individuals and to evaluate and perhaps redefine responsibilities, activities, and values may be heightened when a couple no longer has children at home. Couples may benefit from attending marriage workshops and participating in couples' groups. Table 5 in the Appendix offers a basic exercise that couples can use to trigger discussion.

Widowhood

Having a longer life expectancy than men and the tendency to marry men older than themselves contributes to many women being widowed with advanced years. In fact, by their 8th decade of life, most women are widowed.

The death of the person with whom years of life experiences, joys, and sorrows have been shared can be devastating. Routines are altered...the house seems strange...setting a table for one is hardly worth the effort...rolling over in bed to emptiness is startling. Not only are there adjustments to the routines of daily living, but new skills may need to be gained with the person who handled the checkbook, restarted the furnace, and put air in the tires no longer present. Also, in addition to the loss of companionship, the loss of a significant portion of the household income may be experienced, necessitating changes in lifestyle.

Generally, after the initial grief of their husbands' death passes, most women adjust quite well to widowhood. There tends to be a pool of peers who have shared similar losses with whom friendships can be built. Old friendships may be revived and new interests discovered.

It is not unusual for a widow to have interest in dating or remarriage. In fact, if she has enjoyed a satisfying marriage she is highly likely to develop a relationship with a new partner. This can be challenging, as demonstrated by Sarah's example:

> *Within a year of being diagnosed with pancreatic cancer, Sarah's husband of nearly 40 years died. The couple had married after graduating from college and obtaining teaching positions in the same university. They enjoyed a full social life and raised three children who now had families of their own. In addition to having a solid marriage, they shared a dynamic friendship.*

Sarah wondered how she ever could go on without the love of her life. She would awaken in the middle of the night and get one of her husband's sweaters to hold and smell. More than once she thought she saw his shadow in an adjacent room. Rather than cheer her, visiting family and friends only served to heighten her awareness of her loss.

As the months wore on the pain subsided, although the loss was always felt. When the new school year started Sarah volunteered to work on a few committees and found herself frequently having coffee after the meetings with Craig, another member of the faculty. Craig was a few years older than she, not bad looking, and according to gossip, was divorced for several years. Sarah not only noticed Craig's flirtation with her, but found herself liking it. With mixed feelings, Sarah accepted a dinner invitation from Craig which led to many more dates over the next several months.

Semester break was near and Craig invited Sarah to a long weekend at a resort. She knew there was a strong likelihood that this would afford the opportunity for them to have sex for the first time. She was loaded with mixed emotions. One part of her questioned if this was wrong and dishonoring to her deceased husband's memory; another part of her was excited and eager to explore the feelings that had been stirred. She decided to accept Craig's invitation, telling her family that she was going away on a long weekend break with another faculty member.

Craig's sensitivity and the feelings that had been awakened within her caused Sarah to fully enjoy sex with her new partner. They left the weekend with a deeper commitment to each other and a desire to take their relationship to the next level.

Upon their return, Craig drove Sarah home, unloaded her bags, and gave her a long kiss at the door...just as Sarah's daughter Cathy drove up. Embarrassed, Sarah introduced her daughter to Craig, who left shortly thereafter.

"Mother, what was that all about? You didn't...don't tell me that is who you spent the weekend with," Cathy said with a stern look on her face.

"Yes, you might as well know," replied Sarah, "Craig and I have been dating." He is a great guy and I really feel a connection with him."

"Mother," screamed Cathy, "how can you say that? Daddy hasn't even been dead a year...and at your age. For God's sake, you're a grandmother! For all you know he is after the house and money Daddy left you. You've got to stop this foolishness at once."

Imagine the roller coaster of feelings Sarah experienced. She went from feeling like a desired, vibrant woman to being accused of being an inappropriate old fool. Well-meaning family and friends may react to a widow's new relationship in a less than enthusiastic manner. Sometimes it is due to legitimate concern for the widow; at other times it is due to selfish motives (e.g., protecting family finances, not wanting to lose the time and help the widow offers to them) or stereotypes about what is appropriate behavior for a widow of a certain age.

It is important for a widow to take control of her life and make decisions that serve her well. This is not to say that she is to be oblivious to the concerns. There are unscrupulous people eager to take advantage of women when they are vulnerable. While being discerning, a widow should be open to dating and developing new relationships that can offer her life new experiences and satisfactions.

Divorce

"It would probably be easier if he had died rather than divorce me," said Kay among her stream of tears. Her husband of 36

years came home and announced that he no longer loved her or found their marriage fulfilling, and was moving in with a woman who he believed to be his soulmate. Kay was shocked. Sure, she had recognize that her marriage had become somewhat routine and sex had dwindled to an occasional event, but then, she chalked this up to their being in their sixties. It seemed tensions grew when her husband retired. Suddenly, he was there all the time. When he wasn't complaining about being bored he was disrupting her routines. Finally, he joined a bowling team and spent increasing amounts of time with this new interest. Having absolutely no interest in bowling and her own set of activities to keep herself busy, Kay had no problem with her husband's increasing time spent with his bowling buddies. Little did she know that one of those buddies was an attractive woman 20 years younger than her husband who extended their shared activities from the bowling alley to the bedroom.

Kay's situation is not all that unusual. The divorce rate for people 50-64 has been rising. Some of this increase is related to the transitions that couples face at this stage of life. Spouses who defined themselves through their work role can experience an identity crisis and sense of purposelessness upon retirement. They may disrupt their spouses' routines and invade their territory. After years of being busy with activities separate from each other, spouses may lack shared interests upon retirement. The problems that a marriage may have had all along can worsen during this time.

With divorce hardly an uncommon experience, dissatisfied spouses may not hesitate to end their marriage. If they've been divorced previously, they are at a higher risk for divorce than couples on their first marriage. Aware of the longer life expectancies that they have compared to previous generations, the thought of spending several decades more in an unsatisfying relationship may seem unbearable.

The woman who experiences divorce at midlife or beyond may find that the higher ratio of women to men with each advancing decade limits her pool of potential mates. And of course, there is the tendency for men to seek partners younger than themselves. The divorced woman may have to change her lifestyle to adjust to reduced income and to split assets. Women who do find partners and remarry can face a new set of headaches as issues involving children's acceptance of the new spouse and decisions about how current assets and inheritances among children and grandchildren are considered.

It is wise for women to obtain sound legal advice when going through a divorce. Even when things look straightforward and fair, it helps to have a set of professional eyes review the agreement.

It also is beneficial to seek the support of people who care. Like any loss, divorce can trigger a wide range of emotional reactions that can cloud thinking and lead to actions that could later be regretted. Having the support of friends and family can help to navigate the stormy waters and assist in landing to a stable place.

Parenting

Children are a blessing from God and in that context, the relationship between parents and their children need to glorify God. Parents are the worldly agents for God as they guide and train their children into the roles of godly men and women. This implies that the goal isn't for parents to make children happy or be buddies with them, but rather, to serve their children responsibly by:

- guiding them in understanding that they are God's creation, each made for a unique purpose and possessing a full account of God's love

- exercising authority, setting limits, and disciplining when necessary
- teaching children how to discern and respond to the world in which they live
- helping them to understand not only the mistakes they make, but the underlying reason why the matter is wrong in God's eyes
- assisting and encouraging them to avoid worshipping idols (e.g., expensive clothes, cars, toys)
- demonstrating and asking for forgiveness
- offering opportunities for spiritual growth
- affording opportunities for quality recreational experiences that contribute to their spiritual development
- providing shaping influences within the home of love, service, order, grace, respect, honor to commitments, and reliance on God rather than worldly solutions
- practicing the same pure, unselfish love that God offers them

At midlife, relationships between mothers and children commonly shift from one of caregiving parent and dependent children to interdependent adults. Watching children carve their own paths in life, fall in love and commit to relationships, experience their "firsts", and display their unique giftedness are immeasurable joys for mothers. Yet, graduation from childhood to adulthood is not fairy tale perfect for many children, resulting in anguish, frustration, worry, and depression for mothers. Sometimes mothers can do little to help a daughter see the poor choice she has made in a boyfriend or a son to understand the dead end street he is traveling with his partying friends. Take Marla's example:

Children of the sixties and seventies, Marla and Fred followed the path of many young people of their day in rejecting authority, particularly that which limited their freedom and fun. Marla had been raised in a strict home by parents who professed to be Christians but who lived a life that reflected little of what Jesus commanded. They constantly bombarded Marla with "shoulds" and "should nots" while they fought with neighbors, drank to excess, and displayed prejudice toward people different from themselves. The hypocrisy Marla saw in her parents soured her against anything to do with faith. Fred never knew his father. He was raised by his freespirited mother who encouraged Fred to experience everything in life that he could, including drugs and sex.

When Marla and Fred met in college they were immediately attracted to each other and shortly thereafter moved in together. Marla's parents were outraged that she could "live with a man without being married" which fueled her determination to be with Fred all the more.

In their first year together Marla became pregnant. Although Fred committed to supporting her and sharing parenting responsibilities, there was no talk of marriage. They hardly felt like outcasts, however, because many unmarried couples with children could be found in their college town; it was not only socially acceptable, but quite in vogue.

After college graduation, Fred found a teaching job in a small Northeastern suburb, so the couple relocated. Their new community was quite different from their last one in that traditional family structures and values were prevalent. Because Marla was a stay at home mom with the two children the couple now had, she felt more sensitive to the differentness of her unmarried situation. Her awkwardness was soothed, however, by Ann, a neighbor her own age who also had two small children. Ann and Marla shared many activities together and in time their conversations deepened to issues concerning faith. As

Ann witnessed to Marla, Marla gained an awareness of what a vibrant relationship with Christ was all about and the difference it could make. Gradually Marla shared her new insights with Fred who listened with interest. Over the next year, Marla and Fred developed friendships with some of the Christian couples in their neighborhood and realized that these people had lives with greater meaning and purpose than their nonbelieving friends. They wanted more of what they tasted and eventually accepted Christ into their lives.

When they accepted Christ, Marla and Fred married and committed to living a life that glorified the Lord. Their 7 year-old son and 4 year-old daughter had the benefit of their changed lives. Fred and Marla were delighted to see their son and daughter active in youth groups and living a wholesome lifestyle.

But in the years that followed the unexpected happened. Their son Mark, who had always been a decent boy, offering them no problems, went to work at an ocean resort during a summer break from high school and in August, notified them that he wasn't returning to school. Fred and Marla were stunned. Although Mark had been rather uncommunicative during the summer, they attributed this to his busy schedule and desire to enjoy the beach. When he refused to come home to discuss the matter, Fred and Marla paid a surprise visit to him. When they arrived, the door to his apartment was open so they walked in. Empty beer cans and scraps of food covered the floor. Marla's college experiences enabled her to easily pick up the scent of marijuana. They heard sounds from the bedroom and entered to find Mark in one bed with a girl and another couple in another bed in the same room. Mark looked like a deer caught in headlights but quickly composed himself and asked his parents to wait outside, which Marla and Fred did.

Sobbing, Marla could barely speak when Mark finally joined them, however, Fred had no trouble expressing his views---loudly and aggressively. "What are you doing?" Fred yelled. "We trusted you and look at what you've done. Drugs, whores, liquor. Do you think the Lord is pleased with this?"

Mark responded with equal anger. "She is my girlfriend, not a whore, and I love her. You two had no right barging in on me like this. I've connected with real people here who are living an exciting, full life. They're decent people who help people in ways that I never saw my Christian friends doing. I don't need your Jesus or those boring Christians in my life. I've carved out a new life for myself and this is what I want. You did your thing when you were young and I have that same right." As Mark spoke Marla and Fred realized the hold that his new friends and lifestyle had on him.

Marla and Fred tried everything they could to convince Mark to come home, return to school, think about things, enter counseling, whatever. They cried, pleaded, threatened, and yelled to no avail. They returned home without their son.

Since that time Marla and Fred have been unsuccessful at convincing their son to come home and to return to his faith. Mark says he doesn't have a need for God in his life. The only time Mark contacts them is when he is in trouble and needs bail money. Mark's drug use has increased and is apparent in his haggard look and disjointed thinking. Marla feels like her heart has been plucked from her chest and spends many nights lying awake wondering what went wrong. She and Fred have let Mark know that he is always welcomed at their home. In the interim, they pray.

The pain that a parent feels in witnessing her child's life go sour is incomprehensible. Yet even in the best of homes, life can unfold in unpredictable and undesirable ways. A parent cannot force an adult child to follow her advice; the authority a parent has over an adult child is limited.

Issues cannot be settled between the parent and adult child alone; steadfast prayer and faith that God has purpose and plans are required. Answers may not come quickly or painlessly...clay often must be pounded, broken, and roughly handled before it is molded into its finished piece of sculpture. The example of the prodigal son (Luke 15:11-32) offers examples of the patience, continued love, acceptance, and forgiveness that God desires for us in these situations, as well as the joy and celebration that are warranted when a lost one returns.

Challenging issues can arise even when a child has followed a responsible path and shared a positive relationship with his or her parents, as Sue discovered.

Sue and Jeff, now in their late sixties, were enjoying a new phase of life in ways unimagined. Jeff had retired and the two of them now enjoyed travel, volunteer work, and increased social functions with friends. Their son and daughter had graduated from college, landed impressive jobs, and married individuals who were great people. With sufficient income to cover their lifestyle and ample activities to stay busy and stimulated, they felt they couldn't want for anything more.

A phone call from their son Matt brought a challenge to their ideal lifestyle. The company Matt worked for was severely affected by a tough economy and closed their doors. With living expenses of a wife, toddler, and new baby, Matt could no longer pay the rent on his home and had gone through the small savings that he had. His unemployment check barely covered basic needs and his hunt for another

137

job was producing no results. Desperate, Matt asked his parents if his family could live with them for a few months.

Sue and Jeff certainly wanted to help and had ample room in their empty nest, so there was no question they would assist. Sue was excited to be able to be close to her grandchildren and when Matt's wife found a job, it seemed to make sense for Sue to care for them. Matt and his wife assured Sue that the babysitting only would be necessary when Matt was out job seeking. It seemed fine to Sue.

At first, Sue and Jeff enjoyed the increased involvement with their grandchildren, but they shortly learned that there was a difference between having the kids for a few hours on a weekend and caring for them on a regular basis. Sue had forgotten just how much energy was required to care for young ones. There wasn't much time or energy remaining for the activities Sue and Jeff had been enjoying as empty nesters.

The months clicked away and it now was nearly a year since Matt's family moved in. Jeff found a job that paid considerably less than his previous one, so even with his wife's income, they hadn't yet acquired ample funds to move. As much as she loved her grandchildren, Sue was feeling resentful that Matt and his wife viewed her as a built in babysitter. The contact Sue and Jeff had with their circle of friends had been reduced significantly, and they had little energy to engage in their own interests after a day of caring for their younger family members. Sue was torn between feeling resentful over losing a lifestyle that she and her husband enjoyed (and felt they deserved!) and feeling guilty because of her feelings.

Many women face situations like Sue at this season of life. Certainly, a parent wants to help an adult child who is facing a hardship; however, for everyone's sake, it is important to think things through and develop some understandings. Questions that could be discussed include:

Will money given to help be a gift or loan?

What times and areas are considered private for all parties involved?

If living in the same home, what responsibilities will each person have?

How long will the help be provided?

What impact will the help provided to a child have on his or her siblings?

What are all the options available to address the need?

As difficult as such discussions can be, they can spare many future hurt feelings and burdens.

Grandparenting

One of the joys many women face at midlife and beyond is the relationship with their grandchildren. Without the daily responsibilities for these children and with the maturity derived from decades of life experiences, grandmothers can enjoy their grandchildren and appreciate the special creations they are. Grandmothers also can offer wisdom, guidance, and assistance that can make a tremendous difference to these young lives. By carving out opportunities to spend time with grandchildren, we can take advantage of opportunities to display God's love and share principles for successful living. These do not have to be highly structured events; often, rich experience can unfold with spur of the moment activities, as once was demonstrated to me:

It had been some time since I had seen my 16 year-old granddaughter, Nicole. Although we lived less than one hour from each other, both of our lives were busy and it was easy for long periods to slip by without having contact. Knowing that Nicole was home from school on spring break, I decided to phone and see if she was available for lunch. This was a last minute plan and I told Nicole if she was available I'd pick her up. "Don't worry about getting fixed up, I told her, as "I look like something the cat dragged in." She agreed to join me.

I had detected what I thought to be crying when I phoned her but didn't pursue it on the phone. However, as soon as she entered the car, I noticed the red eyes and asked her if she had been crying. She shook her head yes and poured out the story of how she had brought home an awful report card yesterday and not told her mother about it until today. Her mother responded by taking away some of Nicole's privileges and grounding her for the next few weeks. Although I wasn't pleased that Nicole was not realizing her potential I resisted the temptation to lecture or chastise her. Instead I listened and asked her what the problems were, what she thought she could do to improve the situation, and what help she may need. Her insights and plans were right on target. She seemed encouraged by my faith in her to do what she needed to improve her grades. Over pizza, we chatted about other issues...boys, parents, clothes, horseback riding, and all the miscellaneous activities of a teen's world.

"Yes Nicole, you did the right thing in telling Jason you wouldn't go out with him if he smoked pot." "You're pretty mature to understand why your mom wants to know who your friends are." "It's great that you're not getting your nose pierced." Here and there, I was able to weave in sound principles as issues arose. There was no agenda,

nothing special... just a capture of teachable moments, a celebration of everyday life, and a demonstration of unconditional love.

Through our grandmother role, we can reflect the virtues we want to instill in the young. The way we invest our time and energy can offer lessons in how we use our gifts and talents in meaningful ways. Our attitudes and actions can help the young to see that older lives can be abundant with purpose, contribution, and joy.

Employment

The season of menopause often corresponds to other changes in a married woman's family that may cause her to seek work outside the home. Often, children are out of the home or old enough to demand less assistance from mom. Tuition expenses may create a need for more family income. Husbands may be at a point in their lives where they are reducing work and exploring volunteer or recreational activities on their own. Women may begin to consider new ways to use the time and energy that they now find available. Returning to careers or pursuing a new career may be considered.

The option of entering the workforce or shifting from part-time to full time employment has the potential to be both exciting and frightening. The challenges associated with new responsibilities can be highly stimulating and contribute to a woman's sense of worth. There is something quite satisfying to doing a job well, whether it is answering the phone is a small office or directing an agency. Work can provide opportunities to make new friends, increase social activities, and have fun. Of course, seeing the fruits of her labor rewarded through a paycheck is a benefit as well.

On the other hand, new stresses accompany work. Having to be ready by a specific time can be an adjustment for the woman who was flexible with her schedule in the past. Dealing with traffic, annoying co-workers, deadlines, and bad hair days are added pressures. And, a working wife does create a different dynamic within the family. She seldom is able to do all of the nice little things that a stay-at-home wife can. The house may not be spic and span at all times and the cookie jar may lack home-made goodies. Husbands and children may have to pick up household responsibilities that aren't at the top of their list of things they love to do. And, there will be times when the woman comes home tired and stressed, not only unable to give a lot to others, but perhaps in need of some TLC herself. Families need to address these issues realistically, talk with couples who have faced both sides of the issue, and reach a consensus regarding the decision. Without reaching a decision that both husband and wife can live with, tension and conflict in the marital relationship can result.

If you've been out of it for awhile, some preparation is needed to enter today's job market. Looking at classifieds, talking to friends, networking with former co-workers, and keeping your eyes and ears open help to realistically assess employment opportunities. You may discover that you need to gain some new skills or take refresher courses to regain credentials. This can feel overwhelming and a little intimidating, so take it one step at a time. If you've managed a household and raised a family, you most likely possess incredible skills and a capacity to learn.

Don't be surprised if there are those who discourage your efforts to work. *Bob makes a great salary, you don't need to work. Do you really want to fight rush hour traffic each day? You know, it's a lot different from when you last were out there.* Some of these people may have good intentions; some may be projecting their own fears; and some may be concerned about what your reduced availability may mean to them. Follow your heart.

If you currently are employed, it is useful to evaluate the meaning of work at this point in your life. The best type of job is one that builds on your strengths and provides more than a paycheck in helping you fulfill your purpose and passion.

If after doing some serious soul searching you find yourself in a job that offers little more than a paycheck, consider a change. Granted, this can be as overwhelming and intimidating as entering the job market after decades of being unemployed; however, looking at yourself holistically, having this facet of your life functioning optimally is no less important that having healthy bodily functions. If considering other jobs within your current field of employment doesn't excite you, consider building on your hobbies or interests. Shirley's example speaks to this:

Shirley had worked as an administrative assistant in a high school administration office for over 20 years. She knew the system like the back of her hand and was well-respected for her competency, yet she felt something was missing. The job had become so automatic that she could do it in her sleep and although the cast of students and teachers changed, the activities remained the same.

With her home nest now empty as her children were through college and more time on her hands, Shirley had taken a jewelry making class with a friend. She loved the opportunity to create original pieces and, to her surprise, she was quite good at it. At her instructor's suggestion she rented a table at a local craft show to sell some of the pieces she had made. Not only did she completely sell out by mid-day, but she had a list of names of people who were interested in buying jewelry from her as soon as she had some to show them.

Shirley did some serious soul searching and realized that she not only loved creating jewelry, but could earn some decent money selling the pieces she made. The income wouldn't be the same as she made with the school, but it could work with the reduced expenses in her life.

It has been five years since Shirley made the leap and she has no regrets. She enjoys expressing her creative side and the interesting people she meets as she sells her jewelry.

Perhaps you are not able or do not desire to leave your current job. Consider how you can adjust it to be more compatible with your purpose and passion. For example, this can take the form of a nurse who has grown bored in an administrative desk job being reassigned to a caregiver position. Or, someone may choose to reduce their work hours to have more time to engage in activities outside work that better serve their purpose and passion. Work consumes too much of your time and energy to be invested in something that doesn't serve you.

A majority of baby boomers plan to continue working after age 60, so older women will have a definite presence in the workplace. Mature women often have valuable expertise to share, both in terms of job skills and life experiences that can benefit younger coworkers. In addition to providing meaningful activity and added income, employment at this season of life can be a significant means of serving others.

Transition as Growth, Not Crisis

Whether sought or resisted, change happens. Accepting and preparing for this reality results in life transitions yielding meaningful experiences rather than crises. Some steps that can aid in this process are to:

- be open to letting go of your old way of being and doing. This will leave an open space for new behaviors and experiences that can prove beneficial to your new season of life.

- be kind and patient with yourself. It is normal to have some anxiety and grief over change and losses. Understand this is normal and give yourself time to process your reactions.
- learn ways of *being* and *experiencing.* Engage in quiet time activities, such as meditation, prayer, and yoga. Develop or increase physical activities. Pay attention to that which is around you.
- stretch yourself. Try doing something that you haven't done before, such as joining a group, taking a class, or extending invitations to people you don't know very well.
- find support. Chances are you know women in your age group who probably are experiencing some of the same issues as you. Invite them for coffee and discuss your feelings, plans, and possibilities.
- avoid being discouraged by others. Some of your female friends may feel a little threatened by your new adventures and (often under the guise of "friendly advice") give you reasons why you shouldn't take certain actions. Likewise, your husband may be jealous of the time you are spending on a new interest or your kids may not like the fact that you are not always available to babysit.
- believe in yourself. By this stage of life you have lived through much and acquired many competencies that equip you to navigate new waters. Trust that you can do it!

Study Questions

1. If you could write the ideal obituary for yourself, what would it say?
2. If you are part of a couple, what 3 values do you and your partner most share and on what 3 values do you differ?
3. Why is it so difficult to tame the tongue?
4. What are your children's strengths and weaknesses? What can you do to reinforce their strengths and correct their weaknesses?
5. Review the story of Marla and Fred and consider reasons for their son choosing the life he has.
6. What factors in society create challenges in developing and sustaining healthy relationships? What are some ways that these challenges can be overcome?

CHAPTER 8

Experiencing Life's Blessings

None are so old as those who have outlived enthusiasm
~Henry David Thoreau~

Caring for your body, stimulating your mind, using your spiritual gifts, and exercising the spiritual disciplines foster holistic health. Certainly this has many positive results for you, such as preventing illness, having ample energy to face the challenges of each day, and enjoying feelings of peace and well-being. Yet, your reasons for caring for your body, mind, and spirit are not just for your own personal benefit, but very importantly, to contribute in meaningful ways as you age and experience life to the fullest extent possible. There are actions you can take to achieve these ends.

Reflecting on Your Life Story

Examining the significant people and events that shaped your life aids in your understanding of yourself and others. One means to accomplish this is to trace your life story. Writing your story helps you to clarify thoughts and reflect on your experiences, and provides a record for you to leave for future generations. Also, by connecting the dots of your life journey you are able to see the various times and ways that God has appeared in your life.

The following provides an outline of some of the historical events in your life that you may want to consider when recording your life story, although there certainly are other approaches that you can take.

Suggested Content for Your Life Story

Family background
- Description of parents, grandparents, significant relatives
- Siblings
- Religious and spiritual beliefs and practices

Childhood
- Birth: where, when, unusual events
- Reasons you were given your name
- Favorite activities, interests
- School
- Friends
- Family dynamics
- Special experiences
- Unpleasant experiences
- Relationship with God, religious activities

Adolescence

- Favorite activities, interests
- School
- Friends; role/position in peer group
- Family dynamics
- Special experiences
- Unpleasant experiences
- Relationship with god, religious activities

Adulthood

- Reasons for career choice
- Various jobs you've held
- Education
- When, how, where you met your spouse
- Feelings about marriage
- Where you've lived
- Family dynamics
- Friends
- Favorite activities, interests
- Special experiences
- Unpleasant experiences
- Relationship with God, religious activities, spiritual growth
- Ways in which God has acted in your life
- Legacy you'd like to leave

You needn't be discouraged if writing is a challenge for you. There are other means to document your life story, as is exemplified by Doris, a friend of mine:

Doris has lived a vibrant Christian life for over six decades and had rich life experiences that ran the full continuum of good and bad, righteous and sinful, gut-wrenching and joyful. Her own difficulties and lessons, coupled with a love for the Lord and His people, led her to develop a lay counseling ministry in which the sharing of life stories helps people to learn, grow, and heal.

Through the years, many people who have heard Doris' story urged her to write it, believing it had the elements of a fascinating book. Unfortunately, Doris despised writing, despite knowing that her experiences could minister to others who could learn from her journey. Finally, a friend found the solution and convinced Doris to spend a few days at the beach where they could videotape Doris' story. It worked! Doris unfolded her life story as her friend, armed with her camcorder, recorded and guided her with key questions. Her friend then reviewed the tapes and typed the highlights, providing Doris a document from which to work.

Don't be surprised if reflecting on your life stirs emotions---some of which may be uncomfortable. Surfacing and facing some of the lingering pain, resentments, guilt, and unfinished business may be necessary in order to move ahead.

A review of your life story not only surfaces uncomfortable feelings, though. There can be tremendous joy in reminiscing about your childhood or special---and even ordinary---experiences in your life. You may realize that a friend or relative has woven a thread through your life in a special way, coming to your aid when needed or showing you different facets of life; this awareness could stimulate you to express your appreciation to that individual in a manner you hadn't considered before. Recognizing the obstacles you've overcome, you may take delight in your blessings.

Purpose

What is your purpose? Perhaps you haven't given this much thought, or maybe you define it by the priorities facing you at the time, such as being a parent, earning a living, or singing in the church choir. Certainly, purpose can be realized through these avenues, but it may be useful to consider if you are truly realizing *God's purpose* for you through these activities. Consider Kathy's example:

A bright young woman, Kathy had no difficulty being accepted to medical school. This was an important step toward accomplishing her primary goals in life: being a physician, wife, and mother.

While finishing second in her class and managing a grueling internship, Kathy became engaged to Jeff, who attended the same church. Jeff supported Kathy's career and also was interested in having a family. The couple knew that Kathy's demanding career and Jeff's as a pilot for a major airline would pose unique challenges, but they committed to looking to God for guidance and trusting that He would show them the path to take.

The couple married and enjoyed the new level of their relationship, despite the hectic schedules they both worked. Both of them were achieving success at their careers and earning impressive incomes which allowed them to buy a large home, give handsome donations to the church, and indulge in their passions of skiing and golf.

As planned, Kathy became pregnant after 4 years of marriage. Kathy and Jeff had agreed that Kathy would work part-time after the birth of their children and that they would hire live-in help. Two years after the birth of their daughter, the couple was blessed with a son.

Kathy was both an excellent mom and a fine physician. In fact, the hospital where she worked was so impressed with her that they offered her a faculty position in the school of medicine. As Kathy considered this offer, a colleague told her of a new inner city clinic that was in need of medical staff. "You'd have so much to offer," he pleaded to Kathy. "The community is so medically underserved and could really benefit from having a physician like you as part of the team. Plus, you could plan your own schedule and work whatever hours you'd want."

Kathy realized that a part-time faculty position would yield considerably more status and money than the clinic position, yet there was something about the clinic position that called to her. She visited the clinic and saw firsthandedly the needs that existed. At home that evening, Kathy shared her dilemma with Jeff. "Jeff," she stated with exasperation, "why am I even considering this? The higher salary from the teaching position could enable us to save for the kids' college expenses and put away a little nest egg."

"Kathy," Jeff responded, "this shouldn't be about the money. We've been blessed by being able to pay off most of our mortgage before the kids came along and even with a reduced salary, our income still will be more than enough. Maybe we'll have to forfeit a few expensive vacations and trinkets, but if this is where you're called to be, you've got to go with it."

After considerable thought and prayer, it became clear to Kathy that she needed to take the job in the clinic. And what a great choice it was for her. She sees the difference she can make in lives and feels blessed that she has been given gifts and talents to use in serving in this manner. Although there are friends and family members who can't understand why she forfeited a prestigious teaching position for the unglamorous work in a hectic inner city clinic, Kathy has satisfaction in knowing she is in line with a higher purpose.

Kathy discovered peace and fulfillment by accepting the call to fill God's purpose for her. Although some people may question why Kathy is forfeiting an impressive income and career move, and even charge that she isn't thinking about the best interest of her family, by following her call, Kathy is offering her children a priceless gift in the example of service to others and trust in God to provide.

So, how can you know your purpose? Consider asking yourself what activities:

- express your reasons for existence?
- do you love to do?
- have been confirmed through prayer?
- you'd do whether or not you excelled, got paid, or received recognition?
- bring you a sense of peace?
- have brought about positive results?

It is important to understand that brokenness, pain, and hardship can be used to help you to achieve your purpose. Through hardships and weaknesses you can become more compassionate, pliable, and open to serving. One only needs to read the book of Job to appreciate this. Likewise, your purpose may not be readily apparent, and you may be placed in various situations to prepare for the purpose intended for you. Consider the life of Joseph (Genesis 30-50):

Joseph was bright, and of his father's, Jacob's, twelve sons, he was the favorite. With his self-assured air, he shared a dream in which he saw part of the vision God had for him, which included ruling over his brothers. His youthful immaturity led him to boast about

153

the wonderful designs God had on his life, rather than to seek God's guidance and timing. Needless to say this fueled his brothers' jealousy and anger toward him. Although his brothers initially plotted to kill him, Joseph was spared from death and sold as a slave. This experience was part of God's molding of Joseph, and Joseph was put in charge of his master, Potiphar's, household, thereby providing him with the experience that he would need for the responsibilities in his future.

However, there was another twist in his journey, as Potiphar's wife, angered by Joseph's rejection of her sexual advances, reported to her husband that Joseph had attempted to seduce her, resulting in Joseph being placed in prison. Although Joseph probably had times when he scratched his head wondering what God was doing to him, he remained faithful. When he overheard the Pharaoh's chief cupbearer and baker discussing a dream, he interpreted it for them, using it as an experience to glorify the Lord rather than to promote his own talents. The soon to be freed cupbearer agreed to explain Joseph's innocence to the Pharaoh to assist in Joseph's release, yet failed to do so for two years. Still, Joseph trusted God and remained faithful. Finally, an opportunity came for the cupbearer to tell the Pharaoh about Joseph when a dream interpreter was needed. Pharaoh was so impressed with Joseph's wisdom and discernment that he put him in charge of Egypt. In this position, Joseph was able to demonstrate his capabilities, saving the Israelites from famine. Through his reliance and faithfulness to God through what probably seemed like senseless ordeals, Joseph was able to be prepared for a significant leadership role that secured the survival of God's chosen people.

Like Joseph, you too must be faithful and patient, recognizing that everything that happens in your life is preparing you for your unique purpose.

Following God's purpose for you doesn't mean you need to avoid secular employment or take a vow of poverty. You can use your gifts in any setting or as part of ordinary daily activities. Living a life as a person of faith is to realize purpose wherever you happen to be at any time---often by living an ordinary life in an extraordinary manner.

Vision

With clarity of purpose you can develop a clear mental picture, or vision, for how you want to see your life unfold. Consider the activities that would inspire or excite you. Perhaps you see yourself leading a women's Bible study in a local prison, turning your hobby into a part-time business, or seeking a job in a new field.

Beware of the little voice in your head telling you that you can't. When it emerges, take time to consider the rich experience your years of living have offered to equip you for your new adventure. Connie is a good example:

> *Except for 10 years when her children were young and she stayed at home, Connie had worked as a pharmaceutical company representative. She enjoyed her work and achieved impressive success. Then, quite unexpectedly, the company was sold and she was among the employees terminated when downsizing occurred. Nearly 60, Connie wasn't exactly sad to cease the demanding schedule and travel, but was somewhat anxious as to what she would do. In giving it thought, Connie realized that the one consistent interest throughout her adult life was collecting antique dolls. She loved hunting for them and handling them. "Why not start a part-time antique doll business?" she thought.*

At first the idea sounded silly, but as she gave it serious consideration she realized it was not all that unrealistic. She had knowledge of the field from her years of collecting and knew where to buy and sell. In addition, her years in the business world exposed her to marketing and budgeting principles. It seemed a matter of applying her knowledge and skills to a new area—one that she loved.

Steadily, Connie's business grew. She realized that she didn't want to be confined to set hours so she chose to sell her dolls at antiques shows and online. While not making the salary she once did, she has enough to cover her expenses and engage in an activity she enjoys, at a pace that she chooses.

Connie trusted her intuition and judgment and turned a hobby she loved into a meaningful work activity. Is there an interest or skill that you can build on? If so, envision it and develop a vision statement. Some useful steps to developing your vision statement include:

Developing Your Vision Statement

- *Be specific.* For example, rather than a broad statement such as "help poor children", narrow the statement to "create an after school tutoring program for elementary school children in the eastside of the city." Of course, be flexible. If an opportunity to create the program in the eastside of the city isn't available but one is in central city, that could work.
- *Be proactive and in the present.* Rather than statements like "I hope to tutor children in the city" or "I feel it would be a good thing to volunteer to help tutor kids", state "I am going to tutor inner city children."

- *Push yourself.* Don't be afraid to take a risk and extend beyond your comfort zone.

- *Be realistic.* If you're 76 years old, never played a musical instrument, and envision yourself giving a piano concert at Carnegie Hall, chances are you aren't going to achieve your dream. You could, instead, state that you are going to play Christmas carols on the piano at the family party next Christmas.

- *Own it.* Follow your own desires and passion, even if others don't understand or accept them. You are selecting a destination in your own life journey.

- *Write it.* Putting your vision in writing and placing it in a location where it is regularly seen gives it some legitimacy and keeps it in front of you.

- *Share it.* Telling trusted family and friends about your plans can aid in giving it legitimacy and holding you accountable.

- *Show yourself grace if it doesn't materialize as planned.* There are times when things don't work as planned even with the best efforts. Don't be hard on yourself if this should happen. Regroup, tweak your plans, and try to get back on course.

Celebration

I remember trying to speak to an atheistic relative about the significance of having God in his life. As soon as he realized what I was talking about he stopped me and said, "Look, I may be interested in that stuff when I'm older, but now I'm in my prime and not ready to give up my good times." His reaction was similar to many people who believe that a decision to commit to God implies a solemn, plain, and boring lifestyle. Unfortunately, the flames of this man's attitude have been fanned by some people of faith who are more focused on rules, rituals, and restrictions than a dynamic, authentic relationship with the Lord.

There is nothing in the Bible that says you must forfeit pleasure and joy for God. Quite the contrary! He invites you to make a joyful noise unto Him, rejoice and be glad, and live an abundant life. The Bible is sprinkled with examples of feasts and celebrations. Paul proclaims that the kingdom of God is about righteousness, peace and *joy* in the Holy Spirit (Romans 14:17). Joy often is commanded in the Bible:

Sing joyfully to the Lord (Psalm 33:1)
Be joyful always (1 Thessalonians 5:16)
Rejoice in the Lord always. I will say it again, Rejoice! (Philippians 4:4)

In the rational, sophisticated, and achievement-oriented world in which you live, playfulness, joy, fun, and celebration may seem to be an afterthought or described as achievable only through the latest car, movie, or resort. Yet, God wants you to have pleasure through a relationship with Him. A joyless life hardly is a testimony to the Lord.

Celebration begins with a realization of your blessings. Often, we forget that just having food to eat whenever we desire, clothes on our back, and a roof over our head make us better off than most people of the world. Take a few minutes and think about the answers to these questions:

- What 3 blessings have you experienced in the past week? (These can include simple things in your routine day, such as a friend willing to run an errand for you on a day when you weren't feeling well.)

- What 3 blessings have you experienced in this past year?

- What major blessings can you recall when reflecting on your entire life?

You may be surprised to see that you have been blessed more than you realize. Show your gratitude by joyfully offering praise for these blessings.

It also is useful to reflect on those individuals who have touched your life and develop a written *gratitude list*. List the way the person has blessed your life and then plan some ways that you can express your gratitude. For example:

Person	Blessing offered to me:	Plans to show my appreciation:
Aunt Irene	*Patiently listened to me during times when I questioned the existence of God;* *Regularly sent me inspirational books to mold my thinking*	*Send her a letter thanking her for her support and patience;* *Send her books that now inspire me with notes*
Mom	*Unconditional love;* *A secure and safe home*	*Tell her how much I appreciate her;* *Create a scrapbook of her life for each of her grandchildren so that they will know about this special lady*
Nora, my neighbor	*Does dozens of little things for me without fuss or fanfare*	*Plant a tree in Nora's backyard in honor of our friendship*

Expressing gratitude is a form of celebration that enriches the hearts of others.

Create celebrations to make ordinary days special. My husband holds this wonderful memory of a "celebration" that his mother once created:

> *George's family lived in a townhouse in a community of many children. During a snowstorm, the neighborhood kids were eager to be playing outdoors but without open fields and hills, their options were somewhat limited. In the midst of brainstorming with his friends on what they could do, George noticed his mother intently moving the snow about in their small backyard. She leveled a large area and then began wetting it with the garden hose. "What was she doing?" he wondered. Not long thereafter, she called to him and his friends, "Hey guys, you want to skate?" Although embarrassed by what he perceived as another one of his mother's crazy ideas, George couldn't help but notice that his friends took interest and began migrating to his backyard. Before he knew it, the yard was packed with kids, skating, sliding, and slipping on the makeshift ice rink, having a ball. George's father then set up the grill and cooked hotdogs. Neighbors, seeing the activity, came with cookies, pots of hot chocolate, and whatever else they had to share. The creativity shown by George's mother led to an unplanned celebration that resulted in a special bonding of neighbors… and a warm memory that remains with her children long after her death.*

Consider the way in which you celebrate your birthday. As a child you may have had birthday parties in which you and significant people in your life engaged in a party that set the day apart from others. With the years, birthday celebrations may have been toned down or eliminated, except for the landmark decade points. At midlife and beyond, each year of life lived is a gift…one that not all people are fortunate enough to have.

That alone should give good reason to celebrate the occasion in a special way.

The nourishment of the spirit through the act of celebration gives strength to life and enables you to put events in perspective. It is a proactive means to instill wholesome fun into life. Without this, a void can exist which could be filled by negative influences. Women often are so focused on meeting the needs of others that they don't take time for personal celebrations (or they feel guilty when they do!). If it has been some time since you engaged in a celebration, get out your calendar and schedule one...and be sure it is a responsibility that appears on your calendar regularly! It is significant to keeping your batteries charged so that you can stay in top shape and be your best for yourself and others.

Service

Deeds do not substitute for a vibrant relationship with God or a life lived according to God's will. However, service is an important part of experiencing life's blessings. The discipline of service is for the glorification of God, not for personal recognition and reward. And, it is indiscriminate in that you do not choose to serve in situations that are necessarily fun and fulfilling for you. Let me share two examples from a ministry in which I served.

Faith in Action was an interfaith volunteer caregiving ministry that provided emotional and spiritual support and chore assistance to elderly and disabled individuals. It provided opportunities for Christians to demonstrate their love for the Lord through service while providing assistance to persons who may otherwise not be able to receive the help and support they need.

161

On one occasion, a woman with grown children signed on to volunteer and was assigned to visit an older lady who needed someone to visit, run errands, and do minor chores that she no longer was able to do on her own. After a few visits the volunteer phoned and asked if she could be reassigned.

"What is wrong? Was there a problem" I queried.

"Well, no, not exactly," she responded. "It's just that this lady wasn't all that interesting, and she wanted me to do things like dust her furniture. I don't even dust my own furniture," she exclaimed.

During this same time another volunteer, Andy, joined the ministry---a well-polished, energetic man with an active family, car dealership, and busy life. He was assigned to visit a man who was quadriplegic and could do little else than talk. The intent was to provide this disabled man with someone who could visit periodically and talk about "guy stuff." The relationship unfolded into a very special one, and in a short time, Andy was taking this wheelchair-bound man to baseball and football games, which required that he transport the gentleman in his special van, negotiate a wheelchair through crowded stadiums, and manage the special needs that arose during their time together. Andy continued to make time and space in his life to visit this man regularly for years with few people having any idea of the wonderful act of service he was displaying.

Andy had the heart of a servant in his volunteer experience. He put the needs of the disabled man he served ahead of the personal inconvenience and sacrifice of time he could have been spending on other activities. He didn't get embarrassed when he would draw stares as he pushed his wheelchair-bound friend in public places. He didn't care that he was investing time and energy in something that didn't advance his economic or personal status, or even provide some pleasure for himself. He wasn't at all concerned that few people seemed to know of his volunteerism. Andy had a servant's heart and served as he was called.

What does it take to have a servant's heart? It is an attitude, a way of being. A servant is:

- interested in the needs of others
- empathetic
- open to learning about others
- a good listener
- willing to sacrifice time, energy, resources
- a good steward of the gifts and talents with which he or she has been blessed

A person of faith demonstrates a servant's heart in every domain of life---family, church, work, and play. In some circumstances, this may involve major actions, such as giving a large sum of money to a coworker whose house has been destroyed by fire or committing to a long-term mentoring relationship with a troubled teenager. At other times, it can entail being a blessing to someone in a small way---such as carrying an extra workload on a day that a coworker is not feeling well or helping the young mother with several children carry her groceries to her car.

Being a servant tends to run counter to society's norms. The not so subtle message conveyed through the popular media and lifestyles of those celebrated by the secular world is that *if it feels right for you, you have a right to do it.* We witness examples of corporate raiders making millions of dollars while destroying the jobs of the average worker; celebrities having babies out of wedlock to satisfy their parental stirrings without consideration of the best interests of their children; political leaders violating their marital vows and the dignity of public office by having serial affairs. In a climate of self-gratification, putting the needs of others ahead of oneself seems ludicrous. Yet, loving others as much as we love ourselves is exactly what people of faith are commanded to do. It is one of the areas where the rubber meets the road in our spiritual walk.

Study Questions

1. What do you believe to be your *purpose?* Do you have ample opportunities to express your purpose?

2. How have hardships in your life contributed to the development and expression of your purpose?

3. What prevents people from recognizing and expressing gratitude to those who have touched their lives?

4. Do you express gratitude freely and often? If not, why not?

5. What do you do for fun?

6. How do you differentiate pleasure, happiness, and joy?

7. How does the popular media offer examples of *joyful* lives?

8. How do you celebrate your birthday?

CHAPTER 9

Women Afire: Called to Cast an Enlightened Vision of Mature Women

I want to be all used up before I die.
~Helen Hayes~

*O*ver *the hill...haggard...old crone...wrinkly...out to pasture....* There are probably other less than complementary adjectives that you've heard to describe women at midlife and beyond. Typically, judgments like these arise from superficial evaluations of women based on worldly values of physical beauty, youthfulness, income, and a frantic pace of activity. For too long, women have accepted these judgments. True, ageism---society's stereotyping and prejudice against older people---has influenced the way in which aging women are viewed, yet, we women must accept some of the responsibility. Unlike other groups that have been the object of discrimination, aging women have not spoken out and drawn attention to the problem. Instead, we have meekly sat on the sidelines or withdrawn from the mainstream, suppressing the decades of rich life experience and wisdom stored within us. The unspoken prejudice against our age often leads us to defer to attractive, assertive and less qualified younger people. We not only throw in the towel, but also pull the covers over our heads to spare ourselves ridicule and rejection. Or, at the other extreme, we subject ourselves to plastic surgery, sport clothes designed for co-eds, and spend our energies chasing the elusive butterfly of our fading youth. The time has come to change these unhealthy and unbiblical patterns. We can cast an enlightened vision for mature women that honors their worth based on meaningful, intrinsic values, not superficial secular ones. Through our communication, buying habits, and investment of time and energy, we need to make positive and powerful statements about our maturity. (Keep in mind that maturity implies a ripening, perfection, fullness of development!) Our willingness to heed the call to share a vision that can change the roles and respect for aging women is the goal of Women Afire.

Transforming the View of Mature Women

There are many women hurt, aimless, depressed, disappointed, and thirsty for lives of meaning who are building their lives on quicksand and chasing worthless idols. Imagine how Women Afire could serve these women by bringing them to the well of abundant life and introducing them to the strongest possible foundation on which to build their lives.

Take advantage of opportunities to connect with women one-to-one to discuss the potential for mature women to experience life more fully and make significant contributions. Learn about the women with whom you want to share your vision and address their interests and needs. I have learned that many women who approach me for advice about menopause are most interested in the management of symptoms. *What can I do about these hot flashes? How can I lift this dark mood that I live with? Is there anything that will help me to get a good night's sleep?* These women could benefit from having an enlightened vision of their lives and they certainly have a wealth of gifts and talents that could be used to make a difference in other lives. Yet, if I ignored their requests and began talking with them about vision, purpose, and service, they would most likely become frustrated or even angry. They will not be able to hear the message as they are on one shoreline and I'd be on another. To be effective, I will need to meet them were they are and build the bridge from there that will connect our shorelines.

Ask questions and listen. Provide them with information and refer them to sources of help when necessary. Most importantly, be available and be a friend. Take them to lunch, spend time with them, listen to their problems, send them encouraging notes, share inspirational books. Show them you care and that you love them. As your relationship deepens, share your own life stories. Discuss that God's vision for us is not defined by age or appearance. Help them to identify and use the gifts they possess.

You have opportunities to impact groups of women. Perhaps you lead a Bible study, belong to a women's organization, or work in an office with other women. Formally and informally, you can introduce discussions of the role and potential of women at menopause and beyond. Questions that could stimulate discussion include:

- What impressions of mature women do you see in the media?
- Why does our society seem to value youth over maturity?
- What are some of the messages conveyed via advertising that imply women should fight the normal aging process?
- Who are some women, past and present, who made contributions in their mature years?
- What strengths do mature women possess?
- Why do women buy into society's values about what makes a woman significant? What can they do to change this?
- What does it mean to be fruitful? How can women be fruitful as they age?
- How could the attributes of mature women be used to make the world a better place?

Increased awareness of the injustices to mature women could influence change. A movement could be launched to challenge advertisers, employers, television producers, clothing manufacturers, and other groups to honor and address the realities of mature women. More importantly, a spiritual movement could be fueled in which women of faith demonstrate purposeful lives, defined by God's standards. And, we have several biblical examples to model. Like Sarah we can follow God's lead to accomplish what we thought to be impossible. Like Deborah, we can be wise leaders, advisors, and counselors. Like Lois, we can mentor the young and prepare them for God's work. Like Dorcas, we can use our skills and experience to provide for others. Like Naomi, we can provide guidance and encouragement to younger women.

Not to be overlooked is the importance of living the vision we desire to cast so that we may leave a lasting positive impression. In the urban neighborhood of rowhouses where I was raised, there was a woman by the name of Helen Johns. Helen always dressed impeccably, behaved like a lady, and was consistently pleasant and cordial. But, what I remember most about this special woman was the scent of her Coty L'Origan perfume. When she stopped to chat my senses were delighted by her scent, and long after she walked away the fragrance of her perfume lingered. As Women Afire, we potentially leave a lasting scent wherever we go.

We must live our vision for ourselves, not just through our works but through our characters. There can be tremendous effects by the ripples created as our transformed lives touch our mothers, daughters, sisters, granddaughters, and friends....and their transformed lives touch others. Women Afire can rewrite the life script for aging women and create a final life chapter that is purposeful and powerful.

Breaking from the Cocoon

Butterflies are spectacular creatures. They travel across considerable spans of land, resting here and there, dotting the landscape with vibrant colors. The beauty and wonder they offer are possible because they broke from their cocoons.

Mature women easily can find security in their cocoons. By doing so, they avoid the prejudice of those who superficially see beauty and worth in terms of chronological age and physical appearances. They can spare themselves the effort of having to change and grow. They can minimize painful disappointments. By redecorating their houses for the umpteenth time, meeting friends for shopping and lunch, and selectively volunteering for "fun" projects they weave a thicker layer within their cocoons that protects and isolates them. But the same casing that nestles them in the comfortable known also imprisons their potential and purpose. Unless we break from our cocoons others will not experience what we have to offer.

171

May we be invisible no longer; let us become Women Afire to launch a movement and help legions of women recast the vision for the menopausal years and beyond. It is time to spread our beautiful wings and fly.

Study Questions

1. What have been the effects of feminism on women's lifestyles and family relationships?

2. What is your life producing? What would you like it to yield?

3. What legacy would you want to leave behind?

4. What would facilitate your ability to be a Woman Afire? What would limit your ability?

5. What are three ways that you could cast an enlightened vision of mature women?

Appendix

Table 1 Vitamins and Minerals

Fat Soluble Vitamins

Vitamin	Function	Source
Vitamin A (Retinol)	Antioxidant. Promotes nonspecific resistance to infection, aids in production of lysozymes in tears, saliva and sweat that help fight bacteria, stimulates cell-mediated and humoral immunity, promotes good vision and healthy tissue and hair. Beta-carotene metabolizes into vitamin A in the body and is a stronger antioxidant than vitamin A; at least 15mg of beta-carotene daily is recommended.	Milk, butter, liver, green and yellow vegetables
Vitamin D	Promotes strong bones and teeth, calcium-phosphorus metabolism	Sunlight, egg yolk, organ meats, fish

Vitamin E	Antioxidant properties that aid in the prevention of free-radicals, enhances antibody production, maintains circulatory system; stronger immune-boosting effect when taken with selenium	Dark green vegetables, eggs, liver, wheat germ, vegetable oil, oatmeal, peanuts, tomatoes
Vitamin F (Unsaturated fatty acids)	Promotes healthy skin, blood coagulation, cholesterol, glandular activity	Sunflower seeds, vegetable oils
Vitamin K (Menadione)	Blood clotting	Green leafy vegetables, yogurt, molasses

Water Soluble Vitamins

Vitamin	Function	Source
Vitamin B1 (Thiamin)	Promotes resistance to infection, primary immunoglobulin response, digestion, cardiovascular function, energy production	Peas, lima beans, asparagus, corn,. potatoes, blackstrap molasses, brown rice, meat, nuts, poultry, wheat germ
Vitamin B2 (Riboflavin)	Along with other B-complex vitamins, helps to maintain mucosal barriers that protect against infection, aids in production of antibodies and red blood cells, skin repair	Brewer's yeast, broccoli, spinach, asparagus, Brussels sprouts, peas, corn, blackstrap molasses, nuts, organ meats, whole grains
Vitamin B6 (Pyridoxine)	Promotes health of mucous membranes and blood vessels, involved in antibody formation, red blood cells, affects immune function more than other B-vitamins	Bananas, avocados, carrots, kale, spinach, sweet potatoes, apples, wheat germ, grains

Vitamin B12 (Colalamin)	Development of red blood cells, maintenance of nervous system, believed to exert regulatory influence on T-helper and suppressor cells	Cheese, fish, milk, milk products, organ meats, eggs
Niacin (Niacinamide B3)	Convert food to energy, healthy skin, nervous system, cell metabolism	Cereals, yeast, lean meat, liver, eggs
Biotin (Vitamin H)	Metabolism of protein, carbohydrates, and fats, healthy skin and circulatory system	Egg yolk, green leafy vegetables, milk, organ meats
Vitamin C (Ascorbic acid)	Antioxidant, wound healing, healthy gums, believed to promote phagocytic function, believed to aid in preventing common cold and influenza	Citrus fruits, berries, green peppers, broccoli, Brussels sprouts, spinach
Folic acid (Folacin, Folate, Vitamin B9)	Production of red blood cells, enhance immune system, normal growth	Green leafy vegetables, milk and other dairy products, organ meats, oysters, salmon, Brewer's yeast, dates, tuna, whole grains
Pantothenic acid	Enhances immune system, promotes antibody formation, helps convert proteins, carbohydrates, and fats into energy	Brewer's yeast, legumes, organ meats, salmon, wheat germ, whole grains, mushrooms
Choline (Lecithin)	Regulates liver and gallbladder, cell membrane structure, nerve transmission	Yeast, eggs, fish, lecithin, wheat germ, organ meats, soy
Inositol	Metabolism of fat and cholesterol, nerve function	Molasses, yeast, lecithin, fruits, meat, milk, nuts
Para-aminobenzoic acid (PABA)	Pigmentation of skin, maintenance of hair color, health of blood vessel wall	Molasses, eggs, liver, milk, rice, yeast, wheat germ, bran
Vitamin P (Bioflavoids)	Maintenance of blood vessel wall	Skin and pulp of fruits

Minerals

Mineral	Function	Source
Calcium	Growth and maintenance of teeth and bones, muscle contractions, nerve transmission	Milk, cheese, green vegetables
Chromium	Carbohydrate metabolism, energy production, glucose utilization	Yeast, whole grains, vegetable oils
Copper	Hemoglobin production, enzyme activity, protection from infection	Nuts, seeds, organ meats, raisins, molasses, seafood
Iodine	Production of thyroid hormone, regulation of metabolism	Seafood, kelp, iodized salt
Iron	Transport oxygen to tissues, enzyme activity, immune function	Spinach, lima beans, peas, Brussels sprouts, broccoli, strawberries, asparagus, blackstrap molasses, eggs, fish poultry, wheat germ, shredded wheat
Magnesium	Enzyme activity, regulation of acid-base balance, glucose metabolism, nerve function, protein production	Honey, bran, green vegetables, nuts, seafood, spinach, kelp
Manganese	Enzyme activity in reproduction, growth, fat metabolism	Whole grains, eggs, nuts, green vegetables
Phosphorus	Formation of bones and teeth, muscle contraction, kidney function, nerve and muscle activity	Eggs, fish, meat, poultry, grains, cheese
Potassium	Fluid-electrolyte balance, pH balance of blood, nerve and muscle function	Dates, raisins, figs, peaches, sunflower seeds

Selenium	Antioxidant (with vitamin E), protects cell membrane, promotes humoral immunity, potentiates activity of phagocytes	Butter, wheat germ, whole grains, seafood, eggs, brown rice, apple cider, vinegar, garlic
Zinc	Stimulates T cell immunity (but decreases phagocytic immunity), wound healing, development and growth of reproductive organs, production of male hormone	Brewer's yeast, liver, seafood, soybeans, spinach, sunflower seeds, mushrooms

Table 2
Popular Complementary and Alternative Therapies
and Potential Concerns for Christians

Therapy	Description	Concerns
Acupuncture, acupressure	Based on principles of traditional Chinese medicine, these systems are based on the theory that the body has invisible energy channels known as meridians. *Chi,* or life energy is thought to run through these meridians. Blockages or imbalances of chi can cause symptoms. This can be corrected by inserting needles (acupuncture) or applying pressure (acupressure) at specific points along the meridians. It is believed that the stimulation of acupoints promotes the release of endogenous endorphins that block pain pathways and increases the level of glucocorticoids that relieve inflammation.	Acupuncturists must complete special training and in most states be licensed. Treatments by an unskilled or careless practitioner could result in infection or injury. Some practitioners base their practice on Eastern religions or call on spiritual powers which conflict with Christianity.
Ayurveda	Traditional medicine of India that places equal emphasis on body, mind, and spirit. Based on theory that life is sustained by invisible life energy called *prana* and that individuals have different metabolic body types, *doshas.* When the dosha is out of balance, illness occurs. Uses herbs, yoga, diet, meditation, detoxification, massage, breathing exercises, mental hygiene, spiritual healing, and exposure to sunlight.	Worldviews that conflict with Christianity are used (e.g., Transcendental Meditation to achieve altered states of consciousness, Hinduism overtones). Inclusion of spiritual healing in this system lends itself to practitioner suggesting or imposing non-Christians beliefs.

Biofeedback	System of learning to bring certain bodily functions (such as heart rate, blood pressure, temperature) under voluntary control. Usually an electronic device initially is used to provide feedback of body responses. Eventually, people learn ways to elicit response without use of machine. Not based on any spiritual beliefs or faith systems.	Low risk.
Chiropracty	Specialty that uses manipulation or adjustment of spine and joints to restore alignment. Based on belief that misalignments can cause altered body function and symptoms. Popularly used for treatment of back problems.	Injuries can occur with unskilled practitioner. Some chiropractors may incorporate New Age or other approaches that are not consistent with Christianity, although this is not essential for the therapy to be administered.
Herbal therapies	Use of various parts of plants for medicinal reasons. Can be used internally or externally.	Although natural substances, herbs are not without their risks. They can cause serious adverse effects and interact with drugs. To assure safety and standardized dose, need to be obtained from reliable sources.

Homeopathy	Homeopathic remedies are dilute forms of biological materials (plants, minerals, etc) that produced symptoms similar to that caused by disease. An extract of the substance is made and diluted many times. The more dilute a substance is, the higher its potency. The solution is then added to a sugar tablet, ointment, or other substance.	Low risk. Although remedies can be purchased over the counter, ideal approach is to have homeopath compound remedy based on individual profile and symptoms. Many positive antidotal reports although research is inconclusive as to effectiveness.
Iridology	Examination of eye's iris to diagnose health problems. Based on belief that diseases create visible patterns in different parts of the iris. Different parts of the iris represent different parts of the body.	Low risk, no scientific evidence supporting it. Practitioner may offer products for sale to treat alleged conditions discovered during exam.
Magnetic Therapies	Based on belief that magnets have healing powers due to ability to improve circulation and stimulate nerve endings.	Low risk although should not be used in persons with a pacemaker, who have cancer, or who are pregnant. Some evidence that they could be useful for pain management; little evidence for other benefits, although persons who sell magnet products may make unsubstantiated claims.

Meditation	An activity that calms the mind and promotes relaxation. Can include focusing on breathing, sensations, or specific thoughts; visualizing an image; repeating a word or chant.	If mind is emptied or focus is on something other than God or biblical truths, the mind can be left open to non-Christian spiritual influences. Psychological problems can arise in vulnerable individuals.
Naturopathy	System of health care that uses good health practices and natural means to prevent and care for illness. Emphasize a holistic approach.	Low risk. Some doctors of naturopathy may promote New Age approaches to health and spirituality, although this is not an essential framework for this practice.
Nutritional Supplements	Use of vitamins, minerals, and other nutrients to improve general health and address specific health concerns.	Excess doses of some supplements can be harmful and cause life-threatening effects. Advisable not to exceed recommended dosage range without professional supervision.

Qigong	Practice within system of traditional Chinese medicine consisting of meditation, breathing exercises, and repetitive movements. Aims to unify person with universal life energy. Used for relaxation, stress management, and to promote general well-being.	Practitioners may claim that Qigong can cure illnesses whereas there is no evidence to support this. Life energy that practice is supposed to connect one with may not be God; other religious beliefs may serve as foundation.
Reflexology	Based on theory that areas of the foot and hand correspond to body organs; massage and pressure to these areas can relieve symptoms in the corresponding organ.	Low risk. Few controlled studies to support claims. Some reflexologists may promote Eastern religious beliefs if they consider their actions to be affected universal life energy.
Reiki	Practice of improving flow of life energy by practitioner placing hands on or over 12 different locations and serving as conduit to allow energy to transfer through. Various sensations may be felt by the recipient.	Few controlled studies to support claims. Practitioners may communicate with and draw their energy from spiritual sources other than God.

Tai chi	Exercise consisting of meditation, breathing exercises, and slow graceful movements. Within traditional Chinese medicine, tai chi is believed to enhance and balance the flow of chi.	Low risk. Instructors may incorporate Eastern religious beliefs which are not compatible with Christianity but this is not essential to using tai chi as a form of exercise.
Therapeutic touch	Practice whereby practitioner pass hands over a person's body, several inches from the surface, to manipulate the energy field for the promotion of health and treatment of various health conditions.	Has Eastern mysticism underpinnings which are not compatible with Christianity. Research is conflicting on effectiveness and claimed benefits.

Table 3 Using Drugs Safely

- *Try to address the cause of the symptom rather than just treat the symptom.* For example, if you experience indigestion every time you eat fried chicken and find yourself using an antacid to relieve the discomfort, your wisest action is to omit fried chicken from your diet

- *Use measures other than drugs to treat your symptoms when possible.* Instead of using a tranquilizer when feeling stressed, try meditation, a massage, or deep breathing exercises. If you are having a rise in blood pressure, try changing your diet, practicing yoga stretches, and doing progressive relaxation exercises before starting on an antihypertensive drug.

- *Check for potential interactions.* Inform your health care provider of all the prescription and over-the-counter medications you are using before a new drug is prescribed. Review your medications with your pharmacist and ask about potential interactions. If your are taking any medications on a regular basis, do not begin taking a new drug without consulting with your health care provider.

- *Don't self-medicate or use other people's medications.* It is tempting to use your spouse's unfinished antibiotic prescription when you believe you are experiencing the same ailment or to use the remainder of your antibiotics that have been sitting in the medicine cabinet for over one year, but do yourself a favor and don't do it! Dosage requirements can vary from person to person, as well as from year to year in the same person. Also, drug potency changes as a medication sits. Flush unused prescriptions down the toilet.

- *Follow the instructions carefully.* Don't think that if one works two will work better; in some situations, one can work and two can cause serious adverse reactions.

- *Be knowledgeable of the drugs you are using.* For every drug you use, become familiar with the:

  expected actions

  dosage

  schedule and route of administration

  side effects

  adverse reactions

  interactions

  precautions and

  special instructions

It could be beneficial for you to keep a written record that contains these facts that you can carry in your wallet or purse. This could prove useful in the event of a medical emergency or when you consult health care professionals.

Table 4 Complementary Therapies Promoted for Treatment of Menopausal Symptoms

DHEA (dehydroepiandrosterone): an androgen hormone made by the adrenal gland, available over-the-counter, used to increase sex drive and reduce some effects of aging although research to support effectiveness and safety is minimal. Because levels of natural DHEA in the body decline with age, some people believe that taking a DHEA supplement can help treat or prevent conditions related to aging; however, there is no good scientific evidence to support this notion. Its long-term effects, risks, benefits and safety have not been well studied. Scientists are not certain whether it might increase the risk for breast or prostate cancer.

Soy

Isoflavones (genistein) are naturally occurring compounds that produce weak estrogen-like effects because their chemical structure is similar to estrogen's. Soy products are a popular phytoestrogen (plant estrogen) that are rich in isoflavones. One cup of soybeans contains 300 mg of isoflavone which is the equivalent of 0.45 mg conjugated estrogens. Claims have been made that soy foods offer benefits in reducing menopause-related symptoms and the risk of heart disease. Research suggests that daily intake of soy protein may slightly lower levels of LDL ("bad") cholesterol. Some studies suggest that soy isoflavone supplements may reduce hot flashes in women after menopause, although, the results have been inconsistent.

It is uncertain if soy supplements produce the same benefits as the whole soy food.

Minor stomach and bowel problems such as nausea, bloating, and constipation are possible. Allergic reactions such as breathing problems and rash can occur in rare cases. The safety of long-term use of soy isoflavones has not been established.

Herbs: Claims have been made about the benefits of many herbs in assisting with menopausal symptoms; however, few herbs actually have been proven to have benefit. Also, the risk associated with various herbs are not fully understood. The following highlights guidance from the National Center for Complementary and Alternative Medicine on the use of some popular herbs:

- Rhapontic rhubarb (*Rheum rhaponticum*): research has shown this to significantly reduce hot flashes and other symptoms of menopause
- Black cohosh (*Actaea racemosa, Cimicifuga racemosa*): this herb has been promoted for its estrogenic effect in relieving menopausal symptoms, however, studies of its effectiveness in reducing hot flashes have had mixed results. A study funded by National Center on Complementary and Alternative Medicine and the National Institute on Aging found that black cohosh, whether used alone or with other botanicals, failed to relieve hot flashes and night sweats in postmenopausal women or those approaching menopause. Other research suggests that black cohosh does not act like estrogen, as once was thought. It is advised that this herb not be used by people with liver disorders as it can have very serious consequences.
- Chaste berry (*Actaea racemosa, Cimicifuga racemosa*): believed to affect pituitary function in increase LH and reducing FSH which results in increased progesterone, can take several months to work
- Dong quai (*Angelica sinensis*): some women have reported that hot flashes are reduced and energy enhanced with this

although research shows it to be no more effective than a placebo. Dong quai is known to interact with, and increase the activity in the body of, the blood-thinning medicine warfarin. This can lead to bleeding complications in women who take this medicine.

- Red clover (*Trifolium pratense*): provides isoflavones which have estrogenic effect. There is no evidence that red clover has any benefit in reducing menopausal symptoms. Some studies have raised concerns that red clover, which contains phytoestrogens, might have harmful effects on hormone-sensitive tissue (for example, in the breast and uterus).

- Ginseng: (*Panax ginseng or Panax quinquefolius*): may help with some menopausal symptoms, such as mood symptoms and sleep disturbances, and with one's overall sense of well-being. Ginseng has not been found helpful for hot flashes. (Note: if you are planning to have surgery advise your physician if you are taking any herb that can affect blood clotting; discontinue it several weeks prior to surgery)

- Green tea: strengthens bones, general tonic for good health, not advised for use if you have a clotting disorder or are taking an anticoagulant

The following are other herbs that are popularly promoted for menopausal women:

- Gingko biloba: has been suggested to enhance brain function, but studies have not supported this; not advised for use if you have a clotting disorder or are taking an anticoagulant

- Licorice root: thought to have estrogenic and cancer prevention benefits, but no evidence to support this. Can seriously raise blood pressure
- St John's wort: can improve mild symptoms of depression but has not been proven to be helpful for moderate to severe depression, can increase risk of bleeding
- Valerian: believed to have calming effect and promote sleep. Is being researched by the National Center for Complementary and Alternative Medicine. Studies thus far suggest that valerian is generally safe to use for short periods of time (e.g., 4 to 6 weeks).

Note: Herbs can take several weeks or months to work so patience is needed. Also, knowledge about dosage, effects, and risks is limited because herbs have not been extensively studied. Although natural plant substances, herbs need to be used with the same discretion as drugs.

Homeopathic remedies

Homeopathic remedies are made from minute amounts of plants and other natural substances that produce the same symptoms that you want to eliminate. It is believed that introducing these substances into the body triggers a reaction in which the body develops its own mechanisms for correcting the symptom. For example, if you want to treat a headache you would use a product that is known to produce headaches. This may seem farfetched until you consider that this is the basic principle that is used for vaccines to boost immunity to specific diseases. The process by which these remedies are made is believed to contribute to their benefit also. Although there are many homeopathic preparations available over-the-counter, ideally a remedy or combination of remedies is compounded for each woman, based on her individual symptoms and unique personality. Some common homeopathic remedies used for menopause include:

- Sepia: for fatigue, low sex drive, vaginal dryness, irritability
- Evening primrose oil: to improve function of brain, adrenals, eyes, and reproductive organs
- Lachesis: for hot flashes, headaches, palpitations (particularly useful in women with strong libidos and demanding personalities)
- Pulsatilla: for chills, low sex drive, and low energy)particularly useful for shy, nonassertive women)
- Nux vomica: for nausea, backache, disrupted sleep (particularly useful in women who are perfectionists and who experience chronic anger)

There are no major studies supporting the use of these substances; however, as the substances are derived from natural products and the amounts used in their preparation are extremely small, there is no major concern for serious problems in their use.

Nutritional supplements
- A basic multivitamin that meets the RDAs plus:
  - Vitamin B6 (pyridoxine), 50-500 mg
  - Vitamin C, 1000mg
  - Vitamin E, 800 IU until symptoms improve, then 400 IU
  - Selenium 200IU
- Calcium 1500mg: calcium carbontate type as found in antacids and chews need to be taken with food for best results; calcium

citrate can be taken without food; best to take in divided doses of no more than 500mg at a time; check all sources of calcium intake (e.g., calcium fortified cereals, juices, etc) to determine total intake and do not exceed 2000mg daily as this can cause kidney stones and damage

- Melatonin: 2-5 mg at bedtime to promote sleep

Mind-body therapies
- Meditation
- Progressive relaxation
- Imagery

Acupuncture and acupressure

Acupuncture and acupressure are practices from Traditional Chinese Medicine. They are based on the theory that there are invisible pathways (meridians) that carry energy (qi, chi) through the body. When energy is blocked symptoms develop, therefore stimulating the flow of energy with needles or pressure at specific sites can improve symptoms.

Exercise

Exercise is extremely beneficial in managing menopause symptoms and preventing menopause-related diseases, such as osteoporosis. It stimulates the production of endorphins that improve mood and promotes a better quality of sleep. At least 30 minutes daily of aerobic exercise (brisk walking tennis, dancing, aerobics), weight-bearing exercises (e.g., working with weights, walking), and stretching (e.g., yoga) can offer multiple benefits for menopausal women.

Table 5 Exploring Values in Relationships

Directions: Provide a copy of this list for both you and your partner. Each of you circle 10 words on your list that reflect values that are most important. Compare your lists and discuss differences.

Achievement	Formality
Affluence	Freedom
Ambition	Friendships
Biblical conformity	Frugality
Casualness	Fun
Cautiousness	Genuineness
Career	Growth
Celebration	High stimulation
Change	Honesty
Community	Humor
Compassion	Independence
Competitiveness	Influence
Consistency	Ingenuity
Creativity	Integrity
Effectiveness	Joy
Efficiency	Love
Environmental protection	Marriage
Excellence	Material possessions
Excitement	Obedience
Extravagance	Openness
Faithfulness	Orderliness
Fame	Patience
Family	Peace
Forgiveness	Perfection

Perseverance

Physical beauty

Popularity

Privacy

Purity

Recognition

Relaxation

Respect

Risk-taking

Routine

Secrecy

Security

Self-control

Self-fulfillment

Sensitivity

Service

Sexual gratification

Silence

Socialization

Solitude

Spiritual development

Spontaneity

Stability

Success

Tolerance

Trust

Truth

Work

Worship

EXHIBIT 1
SELF ASSESSMENT OF HEALTH

The following pages offer a comprehensive assessment tool to help you gain insight into your health status. Try to answer the questions as thoroughly as possible as they will help you later when you consider habits that you can acquire to improve your health in a holistic manner.

Self-Assessment of Health

Age_____ Marital status_____ Children_____ Occupation_____

Height_____ Current weight_____ Weight range_____

Diet

Describe your food intake in a typical day:

Describe all items present:

_____Indigestion, heartburn

_____Regurgitation

_____Use of antacids

_____Poor appetite

_____Nausea, vomiting

_____Chronic halitosis

Condition of teeth:

Do you fast? If so, describe:

Nutritional supplements (Vitamins, Minerals, Herbs, Enzymes) used:

   Give amount and type:

Please check the frequency of intake of the following foods:

	Daily	*Sometimes*	*Rarely*	*Comments/Related Factors*
Fruit	_____	_____	_____	
Fruit juices	_____	_____	_____	
Vegetables	_____	_____	_____	
Vegetable juices	_____	_____	_____	
Red meat	_____	_____	_____	
Poultry	_____	_____	_____	
Fish	_____	_____	_____	
Milk	_____	_____	_____	
Cheese	_____	_____	_____	
Pasta	_____	_____	_____	
Bread, rolls	_____	_____	_____	
Cereal	_____	_____	_____	
Beans, peas	_____	_____	_____	
Coffee	_____	_____	_____	
Tea (caffeinated)	_____	_____	_____	
Soda	_____	_____	_____	
Candy	_____	_____	_____	
Cakes, pies	_____	_____	_____	

Ice cream	_____	_____	_____
Chocolate	_____	_____	_____
Salty snacks	_____	_____	_____
Table salts	_____	_____	_____
Sugar	_____	_____	_____
Sugar substitute	_____	_____	_____
Beer	_____	_____	_____
Wine	_____	_____	_____
Hard liquor	_____	_____	_____
Water	_____	_____	_____

Activity

Describe all checked:

_____Difficulty walking or moving

_____Joint pain or stiffness

_____Muscle cramps, pain

_____Muscles too loose, too tight

_____Frequent fractures, sprains

_____Brittle bones, osteoporosis

_____History of falling

Type and frequency of exercise:

Breathing and Circulation

Describe all checked:

_____Allergies

_____Nasal stuffiness

_____Chronic "running nose"

_____Shortness of breath

_____Cough

_____Wheezing, asthma

_____Frequent colds

_____Chest pain

_____Palpitations

_____Numbness

_____Dizziness, lightheadedness

_____Leg cramps

_____Varicose veins

_____History of smoking

Sleep Pattern

Usual bedtime_____ Usual wake-up time_____

Napping pattern:

Do you awaken refreshed?

Insomnia? Describe:

Fatigue? Describe

Sleep aids:

Quality of sleep:

Factors interrupting sleep:

Elimination Pattern

Describe all checked:

_____Urination difficulty, dribbling

_____Pain or burning with urination

_____Voiding during night

_____Inability to pass urine, hesitancy

_____Incontinence

_____Blood in urine

_____Constipation

_____Diarrhea

_____Gas (flatus)

_____Irritable bowel syndrome

_____Blood in stool

_____Hemorrhoids

_____Laxative use

_____Enema use, colonic irrigations

_____Regular   Frequency of bowel movements:

Skin and Hair

Describe all checked:

_____Rashes

_____Itching

_____Unusual sensations

_____Foul body odor

_____Dry skin

_____Oily skin

_____Unusual marks or moles

_____History of shingles

_____Hair loss, breakage

_____Dry scalp

_____Unhealthy looking hair

_____Brittle nails

_____Soft nails

_____Other problems:

Reproductive

Describe all checked:

_____Vaginal discharge

_____Vaginal dryness

_____Hysterectomy

_____Problems with sexual function

_____Change in sex drive, interest

_____Pain during intercourse

_____Breast abnormalities

Perform monthly self-exam of breasts?_____

Date of last mammogram: Date of last GYN exam:

If menopausal:

Year began:

_____Symptoms:

_____Hormonal therapy

If menstruating:

_____Regular menstruation

_____Painful menstruation

_____PMS

Sensory

Describe all checked:

_____Wear eyeglasses

_____Poor vision

_____Cataracts

_____Glaucoma

_____See halos around lights

_____Cloudy vision

_____Pain in eyes

_____Dry eyes

_____Watery eyes

_____Poor hearing

_____Excess ear wax

_____Unusual sensations, tingling

_____Numbness

_____Paralysis

_____Decreased taste

_____Unusual taste in mouth

_____Inability to smell

_____Smell unusual odors

_____Sensitive to scents/odors, describe:

Date of last eye exam:

Date of last hearing exam:

General Symptoms

Describe all checked:

_____Frequent colds, infections

_____Headaches

_____Pain

_____Unusual fatigue

_____Swelling

_____Other:

Emotional and Spiritual

Describe all checked:

_____Depressed

_____Anxious

_____Moody

_____Mood swings

_____Hyperactive

_____Suicidal

_____Episodes of confusion

_____Inability to focus

_____Easily cry   _____Never cry

_____Feel hopeless

_____Paranoid, suspicious

_____Argumentative

_____Passive

_____Difficulty maintaining relationships

_____Marital conflict, problems

_____Difficulty coping

_____High level of stress in life

            Measures to manage stress:

_____Belief in God

_____Read Bible regularly

_____Connection with faith/spiritual communicty

_____Feel spiritually empty, distressed

_____Feel worthless

_____Feel life has no meaning

Changes I would like to make in my life:

Known Health   Treatment/Management
Conditions/Diagnoses

Prescription and Nonprescription Medications Used

Medication   Dosage   Reason Used

Complaints

List major health complaints you have about your health in order of importance:

Landmarks in Your Life History

Often, significant events, positive and negative, can provide an understanding of your current health status and needs. Divide your life into decades and remember the significant occurrences during each decade. These can include the loss of a significant person, change in school or job, relationship started or terminated, illness of self or significant others, period of spiritual growth or distress, etc.

List the occurrences the appropriate decade. (Use additional paper if needed).

Age	Description of Significant Occurrence
1-9	
10-19	
20-29	
30-39	
40-49	
50-59	
60-69	
70-79	
80+	

©Charlotte Eliopoulos

You may feel that completing an assessment such as this one is a tedious process. Perhaps you've never had to participate in such a comprehensive assessment of your health status. Unfortunately, the realities of our health care system are that many practitioners are too busy to spend time getting to know the minds, bodies, and spirits of their clients and insurance reimbursement favors the treatment of symptoms and diseases rather than the nurture and care of the whole person. This presents a challenge for you to be an informed, proactive health care consumer so that you will be able to:

- understand the many influences on your health
- identify problems and relationships among your mind, body, and spirit that may not be readily apparent to your health care provider
- be able to seek the assistance you need from the source best able to help you (e.g., physician, clergy, nutritionist, counselor, etc.)

Now, let's turn our attention to some of the basic needs that all human beings share; these are:

Respiration

Food and water

Elimination of wastes

Movement and exercise

Activity

Sleep and rest

Safety

Normality

Solitude

Purpose

Connection with God, self, other people, nature

These needs seem fairly simple at first glance, but their fulfillment relies on several complex factors, including:

- *Physical, mental, and socioeconomic factors:* A person who is paralyzed and unable to lift a utensil to her mouth or someone who has Alzheimer's disease and cannot remember what to do when food is placed before him may be able to chew, swallow, and digest food, but lack the ability to get food into his or her mouth due to physical or mental impairments. Likewise, a senior citizen on a fixed income may omit the medications that her body needs to function normally, because she lacks adequate funds to pay for the prescription.
- *Knowledge, skills, and experience:* A pregnant woman who is unaware that alcohol can be dangerous to her baby may continue drinking and threaten the safety of her child. A person who lacks an understanding of the significance of a relationship with God may experience hopelessness and depression in an existence without spiritual meaning.
- *Desire and decision to act.* An individual could describe the recommended dietary intake and list foods that are harmful, yet continue to consume junk foods. A person may know that an adulterous relationship is sinful and risks destroying his health, job, and family yet be unwilling to terminate the affair.

Go through your self-assessment and highlight or circle **signs, symptoms,** and unusual or abnormal **habits.** Now, think about the specific need that is affected by the signs and symptoms and write them under the appropriate heading in column A on the form on the next page. Some signs and symptoms can affect several needs. For example, "Use of antacids" can be listed under *Food and Water* and *Safety*; "Unusual fatigue" can be listed under *Movement and Activity, Sleep and Rest, Connection, Safety,* and *Normality*.

Now, examine the signs, symptoms, and habits and try to consider the **underlying reason(s)** that could be responsible, such as *eating a lot of fried foods* for "Use of antacids" and *eating poorly and having stressful job* for "Unusual fatigue." Jot down what you believe the underlying reason to be in column B. In some circumstances, you may not know the underlying reason; it is fine to put a question mark in the column.

Lastly, in column C, write an **action** you can take to change or reduce the sign, symptom, or habit, such as *reduce meals at fast food restaurants to once a week* or *discuss excessive workload with supervisor*. For some signs, symptoms, and habits, your action may need to be to obtain a medical evaluation, seek the counsel of clergy, or pray for insight and guidance into the situation.

Following the blank Action Plan for your use is one that shows some options to consider under each category. You can use some of the health facts discussed in earlier sections of this book to assist you in developing your actions.

EXHIBIT 2
YOUR ACTION PLAN TO IMPROVE YOUR HEALTH

Need	A Sign/Symptom/ Habit	B Underlying Reason	C Action
Respiration			
Food and water			
Elimination of wastes			
Movement and activity			
Sleep and rest			
Solitude			

Need	A Sign/Symptom/ Habit	B Underlying Reason	C Action
Connection with God, self, others, nature			
Safety			
Normality			

Sample Items to Include In Your Action Plan

Need	A Sign/Symptom/ Habit	B Underlying Reason	C Action
Respiration	Chronic cough	Smoking	Enroll in smoking cessation plan
	Shortness of breath when climbing >15 stairs	Poor physical condition	Begin exercise program
			Do deep breathing exercises several times throughout the day
Food and water	Frequent heartburn	High intake of fried food	Eliminate fried foods
		Eat while working- →stressed mealtime	Increase fresh foods, broiled and baked items
	High intake of snack food	Don't have time to go to cafeteria at lunch time; rely on vending machine items	Schedule time to eat in cafeteria
			Keep healthy snack foods in office

Need	A Sign/Symptom/ Habit	B Underlying Reason	C Action
Elimination of wastes	Frequent constipation	Low fiber and fluid intake Low activity level	Include bran cereal at breakfast Eat at least 5 fresh fruits daily Eat a salad at lunch Adhere to exercise program
Movement and activity	Stiff joints in morning Difficult to walk and engage in physical activity	Lack of exercise	Get physical exam to determine safety of exercise program Begin exercise program Park car in farthest space from building Perform yoga stretches several times each day
Sleep and rest	Poor quality of sleep Awake tired, difficult to get out of bed Nod off after meals	High consumption of caffeine Spouse snores loudly Consume high amount of sweets	Eliminate caffeine after 4PM Suggest spouse get evaluated for snoring Sleep in separate room every other night Change diet

Need	A Sign/Symptom/ Habit	B Underlying Reason	C Action
Solitude	No time alone	Care for family 24-7 No money to go away or get babysitter	Housesit for friends when they go away for the weekend and ask spouse or other family member to babysit Negotiate with spouse to have 30 minutes each day to be relieved of childcare responsibilities and take long bath Awaken 30 minutes before family for personal quiet time
Connection with God, self, others, people, nature	Often neglect prayer life	Allow worldly demands to take priority	Discuss with friend and ask friend to hold accountable
Safety	Take higher than recommended doses of medications for headaches Overuse antacids	Fail to manage stress and eat well	Eat healthier diet Practice stress management techniques daily Eliminate foods that trigger heartburn

Need	A Sign/Symptom/ Habit	B Underlying Reason	C Action
Normality	Overweight No interest in sex	High consumption of snack food Tired at bedtime Don't feel attractive due to weight gain	Begin weight reduction diet Begin exercise program Discuss concerns with spouse Plan romantic weekend away with spouse

About the Author:
Charlotte Eliopoulos RN, MPH, ND, PhD

Charlotte Eliopoulos has been a leader in casting enlightened views of aging. A respected and prolific author, she wrote one of the leading texts in gerontological nursing to guide nurses in offering care to aging individuals based on scientific evidence rather than myth, as well as over a dozen other books and numerous chapters and articles related to geriatrics and holistic health.

Through her workshops, Charlotte has equipped women to age with optimal health and inspired them to recognize the significant contributions they can make in their later years. She hopes to see a growing movement of mature women who demonstrate the power they hold to impact society.

To connect with Charlotte, share feedback, and learn more about becoming a *Woman Afire!* visit

www.WomenAfire.com

Made in the USA
Lexington, KY
12 January 2013